Flights of "13MIKE"™

for versions 4.0 and 5.0

A Microsoft®
Flight Simulator®
Companion

by
Professor Fred J. Calfior
and
Professor Douglas W. Miller

Book One - Level A

Covering the Los Angeles, Chicago, San Francisco, and New York areas

Flights of "13MIKE."™

Printed in the U.S.A.

First edition, 1994.

International Standard Book Number: 0-9639052-2-8.

Library of Congress Catalog Card Number: 93-90850.

Microsoft is a registered trademark of Microsoft Corporation.

Flight Simulator is a trademark of Bruce Artwick.

13MIKE and Airienteering are trademarks of CalMil Publishing.

About the Authors

Professor Fred J. Calfior

Fred Calfior is a 1975 graduate from the United States Naval Academy, with a degree in Aerospace Engineering. He has instructed in both the T2C Buckeye (a twin engine jet) and the TA4J Skyhawk (a single engine jet). Upon joining the Embry-Riddle Aeronautical University faculty, Professor Calfior acquired his Masters in Aeronautical Science. He has been involved in all levels of flight instruction, as well as academic instruction, in the areas of Aerodynamics, Flight Performance, and VFR/IFR Navigation.

Professor Douglas W. Miller

Douglas Miller is a Professor at Embry-Riddle Aeronautical University where he teaches Aerodynamics and Electronic Flight Control Systems. Professor Miller has an extensive background in aircraft system design and simulation development. As a consultant to the aerospace industry, he has been responsible for the development of a variety of multi-user simulation systems, including a virtual reality simulation used for vehicle design and analysis. Professor Miller has extensive instrument and weather flying experience. Most of this experience was obtained while flying his Mooney for business purposes. Currently Professor Miller is involved in the research and development of a virtual reality flight simulator for teaching and flight technique analysis.

Other Flights of "13MIKE"

BOOK TWO   (Coming Spring 1994)

IFR Flights of "13MIKE" - LEVEL B

These scenarios are all instrument flights performed in thunderstorms, overcast, night, and day weather conditions. These flights have been created from the wealth of instrument flying experience of the authors. They make you feel like you are right there in real life, fighting the turbulence and weather as you shoot an approach with a 200 foot ceiling at night. **You've got to try this one**!!

BOOK THREE   (Coming Summer 1994)

Airienteering™ with "13MIKE" - LEVEL A

What would it be like to do a little orienteering with an airplane? Well, jump into old 13MIKE, get out the map, and let's hit the sky. We need to find all the marks and get back to our home field as fast as we can. The clock is ticking and it looks like a storm is brewing. How good are you at map reading and flying at the same time? Come fly with 13MIKE and find out.

Order form in back of book

✈ Preface

Professor Miller and I were flying the Microsoft Flight Simulator one evening, having a golden time zipping underneath the Golden Gate Bridge and zinging about on World War II low level missions! We flew the night approach into San Francisco and decided to fly down to San Diego. What we came to realize was there were no canned cross country flights that we could follow. Making one up for ourselves was not very challenging since we already knew all the answers. So began a plan which entailed the development of cross country scenarios, with the ability to challenge any individual. They ranged from easy to hard in areas of navigation, approaches, and landings while at the same time being pure entertainment and fun!

We noticed, as we flew these scenarios, that our skills with the simulator became sharp and we were able to nail the numbers with regularity. It was determined that this was due to a combination of increased dexterity with the controls and the adherence to good flight procedures.

By drawing on our experience and background in teaching flying and flight concepts, we have been able to bring to you a very authentic and realistic set of cross country flights.

This is the first book of a vast series of upcoming companion books to the Microsoft Flight Simulator program. The books have been designed to be flown in sequence, even though it is not required. The companions come in two levels. Level A is primarily visual flight (VFR), keeping the non-pilot and student pilot well challenged but within reach of everyone's flying ability. Level B, on the other hand, is a book geared to anyone who has completed the first book or is an experienced pilot. This book deals with bad weather, overcast, and cloudy instrument flights. It is very challenging and realistic.

This companion is divided into four, area specific, series of flights which can be flown as continuation hops or handled separately as self contained units. The areas are:

Los Angeles, California

1. Riverside to La Verne
2. La Verne to Santa Monica
3. Santa Monica to Torrance
4. Torrance to Avalon

Chicago, Illinois

1. Lansing to Aurora
2. Aurora to Bloomington-Normal
3. Bloomington-Normal to Kankakee
4. Kankakee to Chicago Meigs Field

San Francisco, California

1. Salinas to San Jose International
2. San Jose International to Oakland International

New York City, New York

1. Bridgeport, Connecticut to La Guardia International
2. La Guardia International to Kennedy International

You will notice that there are scoring points throughout the flight scenarios. They are weighted in accordance to their degree of importance in the VFR flying arena. The purpose of the scoring is so you may have a target of proficiency to shoot for . We'll tell you, based upon your score, what category of pilot you **REALLY, REALLY** are! The answers for each scenario are provided in the back of the companion, so that you can tell how close your skills are to whatever goals you've set for yourself.

Flights of "13MIKE" - Book One - Level A has been prepared and written so that it challenges the non-pilot, student pilot, and commercial pilot. It is assumed the student is familiar and versatile with the Microsoft Flight Simulator Versions 4.0 or 5.0. This is not a teaching aid on how to fly the simulator - we assume that you have already practiced using the Microsoft Flight Simulator's own manual and guide. So whether you have version 4.0 or 5.0, this companion provides you with a custom program geared for your needs no matter what version you own.

The airplane in which you will be practicing is a Cessna 182 RG, a retractable gear airplane. We recommend that you use the map display very sporadically - more for curiosity sake than anything else. The areas are default areas which come automatically with your original Microsoft program. You won't have to build any scenery, locations or navaids unless you want to do so for your own personal thrill. We also recommend that you follow all the steps in each scenario so you can build a habit pattern of awareness in procedural techniques, especially in the preflight area. If you do skip a step, you won't fall out of the sky and die in simulation, but you will fail to utilize this companion to its full benefit!

VOR navigation is quite frequently used in your flight scenarios because it is a vital part of VFR cross country work wherever you go. And also because, the ground views of the Microsoft Flight Simulator program are not built up to the extent of capably using them as dead reckoning and pilotage points of reference. The following companion to this one, **IFR Flights of "13MIKE" - Book Two - Level B**, is geared specifically to the IFR environment where you will be flying solely by reference to your instruments.

You may fly each one of these flight scenarios using your keyboard, mouse, or joystick. There is no specific preference. The transfer of learning will be attained by the application and practice of the standardized procedures which are a foundational part of each and every flight scenario. These procedures are practiced and accepted worldwide. We recognize that there will be differences of opinion based upon Fixed Base Operator (FBO) or flight school methods of instruction. For example, the magneto checks which we have you do, are performed with "**LEFT**" first, then with "**RIGHT**" so that at the end of the final magneto check, one click will bring it back to **"BOTH"**. If the **"LEFT"** magneto was checked last, then one click would rest on the **"RIGHT"** magneto, and a pilot could then quite inadvertently take off with only one magneto in operation!

So, start up your computers! **CESSNA 13MIKE** is ready to fly with you to the exciting and challenging VFR world in a totally hands on, you're in control, plan ahead style of airplane navigation! Happy flying!!!!!

****

As you progress through this companion, we would enjoy hearing about your triumphs, thrills, and any other comments you may wish to share with us. We are always eager to hear from our fellow flyers. All comments are appreciated. Please send them to CalMil Publishing, 2224 Katahn Drive, Prescott AZ, 86301.

Professor Douglas W. Miller
Professor Fred John Calfior

Table of Contents

PreFlight

ABOUT THIS COMPANION

The flight scenarios in this companion have been written with the assumption that you are familiar with the operation and control of Microsoft Flight Simulator 4.0 or 5.0.

Hi! My name is Professor Miller. Professor Calfior and I will be helping you fly "N9413M", referred to as "13MIKE" (pronounced "ONE THREE MIKE"), through the scenarios in this companion. It is to your advantage to read the Microsoft Flight Handbook and understand all the keyboard controls for operating the instruments, engine, and flap controls on the Cessna 182 RG instrument panel before starting. An excellent way to acquire this knowledge is by going through Microsoft's "Flight School".

The following Flight School sections are recommended: 1) "Ground School", 2) "Basic Flight Training", 3) "Advanced Flight Training", and 4) "Navigation Course". It is best to complete all lessons in each of these sections. Flying the scenarios in this companion without the Flight School experience is possible. We try to provide as much help as we can in areas where you may run into problems. You can also refer to the Microsoft Flight Handbook for help. We highly recommend that you have a good understanding of how the following instruments work: 1) VOR and OBI, 2) DME, and 3) VSI.

Flight Simulator version 5.0 comments

The latest version of Microsoft Flight Simulator is something to behold. The scenery is fantastic, and the instruments and controls are very realistic. There are a few differences between versions 4.0 and 5.0. We have used a bold square bracket **"[ ]"** to indicate any 5.0 version specific command or answer. **If you are flying version 5.0, please use the numbers in the square brackets.**

You will need to set your propeller to a "**fixed pitch**". Aircraft position will need to be set using **Latitude** and **Longitude** settings. 5.0 also displays NAV 1 and NAV 2 DME simultaneously. When you come across a command that tells you to switch to NAV 2 DME, just revert your attention to your second DME display.

FLYING THE SCENARIOS

"Competitive", "Challenging", "Fun", "Exciting", "Thrilling", and "Nerve Racking" are words that have been used to describe flying these scenarios. Non- pilots, student pilots, and commercial pilots are all hooked on the challenge and adventure of "13MIKE". You do not have to be a pilot to enjoy the thrill and adventure of flying through the LA TCA Corridor and doing a step down instrument assisted approach. Professor Calfior and I help you every step of the way. Professor Calfior is seated at your right for the entire flight. He provides helpful hints, when they are needed, and provides diagrams so you can see what the departure and approach looks like.

The flight scenarios we created in this companion are the results of our many years of actual flying and flight instructor experiences. We hope you will benefit from the great effort we expended to assure the authenticity of each and every scenario, and the realism that we ingrained into each flight.

As you progress through the flights, you will get a sense of repetitiveness from scenario to scenario. Because of the authentic nature of each flight, it was necessary to step through the repetitive procedures that are an inherent part of every real flight. Flight instructors spend hours upon hours trying to get the student to be able to repeat these procedures in their sleep. Welcome to the real world of flying!

Okay, here is an overview of the setup procedures, COM dialog, questions format, simulator flying techniques, and general hints.

SETUP

Aircraft - It is important to select the Cessna 182 RG aircraft. All performance and position parameters are based on the 182 RG. If another aircraft is used, your answers will not match the answers in the back of the book.

Winds - The winds are set by levels. The wind changes speed and direction as your altitude changes. Double check the level settings and make sure that the wind speeds and directions indicated in the SETUP section of the scenario match your settings. Your distance, timing, and position answers will be off if the winds are not set correctly.

Position - When the simulator starts, you are placed at a default airport and runway. Do not be concerned about this. The SETUP section of the scenario takes you through a repositioning series of steps. Just follow the instructions and you will be repositioned at the correct airport for the departure part of the scenario. The aircraft positioning sequence has four parts, "NORTH", "EAST", "ALTITUDE", and "HEADING". Be sure that all parts have been set correctly. You do not need to set the "Control Tower" position. **_Caution_**, your position will be different at each airport. You will need to read the TAXI section to determine how to get to the runup area for the departure end of the runway in the scenario.

COM SETTINGS and DIALOG

This companion is based on realistic flight procedures which include radio communications. Unfortunately, the radio dialog of the Microsoft Flight Simulator is limited, therefore we have inserted full radio communications dialog within the scenarios where they would normally occur. This dialog will appear after you have changed COM frequencies, and a transmission on your part or a broadcast message would normally take place. At times, you will tune in an ATIS frequency and see a message run across your outside view screen. Microsoft Flight Simulator has ATIS broadcast messages at selected airports only. To make the scenarios as realistic as possible, we have included ATIS messages in the companion for all airports that are used. These ATIS messages will not necessarily match those that Microsoft displays. You only need to be concerned with those in the companion.

QUESTIONS and ANSWERS

One of the objectives in flying the scenarios is to obtain the highest score possible by performing the listed procedures as precisely as you can. At different times during the execution of the scenario, you will be asked to "pause" the simulator. Write down specific flight parameters or answer certain questions pertaining to the flight (all questions are indicated with a double "**"). After you have written the information down, you will be asked to continue the simulation. Each question has a certain point value assigned to it. Some questions are more important than others, and therefore have a higher point value. At the end of the flight, you add up the points to find out what kind of pilot you are. You will need to study the questions you missed so you can do better the next time you fly that scenario.

THE PATH TO THE PERFECT SCORE

Obviously, you are interested in gaining the maximum number of points for each flight scenario. The level of flight difficulty increases as you get deeper into the book. For the most part, it will take you at least three to five attempts before you can nail each flight scenario with a maximum score! The harder flights may even require more than five flights! So don't feel discouraged at a low score for your first flight. That's what makes these series of flight scenarios so dynamically alive and heart pounding! You keep trying to better your previous attempt, being ready for a required quick reaction that you may have missed before, or keeping your VOR needle centered so you can accurately meet a checkpoint.

We recommend the following five step sequence when you're ready to fly:

1. READ THE ENTIRE SCENARIO FROM START TO FINISH TO SIMPLY GET A FEEL FOR THE FLIGHT.

2. ENJOY BEING IN THE AIR DURING YOUR FIRST FLIGHT. TRY TO STAY A PAGE AHEAD SO YOU CAN ANTICIPATE WHAT IS COMING UP. GO FROM DEPARTURE TO DESTINATION FOLLOWING EACH SERIES OF NOTES AND TASKS METHODICALLY.

3. THE SECOND FLIGHT, YOU KNOW WHAT TO EXPECT. STABILIZE YOUR FLYING BY BEING SHARPLY ON ALTITUDE - PROPER POWER SETTINGS - RECOMMENDED OR PREVIOUSLY DISCOVERED DESCENT RATES, ETC. SEARCH TO SPECIFICALLY BETTER THE AREAS WHICH YOU MISSED THE FIRST TIME.

4. THE THIRD FLIGHT, SKIP THE PROFESSOR CALFIOR INSTRUCTIONAL NOTES (YOU'VE BEEN THROUGH THEM TWICE NOW!) AND CONTINUE WITH THE RADIO CALLS. HUNT FOR THOSE ELUSIVE CORRECT NUMBERS, BUT KEEP THE FLOW NONSTOP FOR THE ENTIRE FLIGHT RIGHT TO THE LANDING.

5. THE FOURTH FLIGHT AND ANY ADDITIONAL FLIGHTS, PAY SHARP ATTENTION TO ALL THE NUMBERED NOTES. THESE FLIGHTS WILL BE QUITE DYNAMIC BECAUSE YOU WON'T BE NEEDING TO READ AHEAD TO PREPARE FOR THE NEXT STEP! YOU'VE GOT THE SCENARIO PRACTICALLY MEMORIZED. WHEN YOUR TIMING IS ON, AND YOU KNOW THE ROAD, IT BECOMES ONE THRILLING MANEUVER AFTER ANOTHER.

HINTS and SIMULATOR TECHNIQUES

The following is a list of flying techniques that will help in performing the scenarios with more accuracy and precision, thereby increasing your score:

a) You may need to adjust your power setting from the one stated in the scenario. This is due to deviations from the correct approach speed and altitude.

b) Watch your VSI (vertical speed) on approach. Try to maintain a constant vertical speed.

c) Watch your heading. The winds will make your airplane fly a different ground track than your heading would indicate. You may need to set in a crab to compensate.

d) Watch overbanking and over controlling. It is easy to over control the simulator. After putting in a roll control, you will need to put in an opposite control to stop the roll. Do not overdo it. The airplane will oscillate back and forth if you do. Gentle on the controls.

The following hints will help you in flying the scenarios in the beginning. After you become more proficient, try to fly without the aid of these hints.

a) For finding the airport and taxiing around the airport, use the "Num Lock" key.

b) To determine orientation to the airport and other landmarks, use the "Scroll Lock" along with key pad numbers 1 thru 9 (except 5) to change your view of the outside to the different windows of the aircraft.

c) To provide more stability to the aircraft and minimize the aircraft's tendency to wander, you may want to fly with the autopilot "wing leveler" on.

d) To help maintain your orientation to the surrounding landscape, follow your flight on the sectional maps in the appendix.

e) You should fly the scenarios more than once, trying to improve your performance, accuracy, and score each time. Remember timing is important.

f) You may want to save your approach or landing configuration so you can practice these sections without having to fly the entire scenario again.

GENERAL FLIGHT TECHNIQUES
and
RULES OF THUMB

The following section consists of some helpful instructional aids, techniques, hints, and rules of thumb which will allow you to accomplish the basic flight maneuvers given throughout your flight scenarios. It will help you acquire a high flight score.

Takeoff:

The takeoff can be separated into three segments.

1) The takeoff roll   2) The liftoff   3) The initial climb

a) The takeoff roll is simply an acceleration of the airplane to its rotation speed with full power. It is important to maintain the centerline of the runway. As the speed increases to rotation speed, gradually increase back elevator pressure in order to get the weight of the aircraft off the wheels.

b) The rotation speed for the Cessna 182 RG is 50 knots. The aircraft will then continue to accelerate to 70 knots. It will then lift off the ground since there is now enough air over the wing to generate the necessary lift.

c) In the takeoff roll, winds will not always be right down the runway. These crosswinds can make it slightly more difficult to maintain that runway centerline. Proper procedure calls for full ailerons into the wind at the start of the takeoff roll. As the ground speed accelerates, the ailerons are slowly taken out until at rotation speed, they are centered.

d) Once airborne, you need to maintain a specific climb speed. 80 knots is the climb speed generally utilized in these flight scenarios. Since the airplane wants to accelerate very rapidly, you must set about a 10° nose up attitude on your attitude indicator.

e) With liftoff, the nose wants to rise higher than it needs to. That's why a slight nose down pressure may be necessary in order to stabilize a 10° nose up attitude.

f) Let your nose control the airspeed here, since full power is a constant until 1,000 feet above the ground. If your airspeed is greater than 80 knots, raise the nose to bring the airspeed back to 80. If your airspeed is not yet at 80 knots, lower the nose so that you can reach it.

g) Once airborne with a crosswind being prevalent, a "crab" into the wind will be needed to maintain the runway centerline on climbout. Check behind you to verify that you're aligned with the runway, and then use an offset heading into the wind to keep that track as desired.

h) As a general rule of thumb, when you are 500 feet above the ground, then you may retract your flaps to the full up position. (We are assuming that you have taken off with a 10 degree flap down position). When the flaps come up, there is less drag on the airplane and it wants to accelerate. At the same time, the nose wants to drop, which aggravates the stabilized climb speed you have. Therefore, with flaps coming up, consciously raise your nose attitude a bit to keep a hold of your 80 knot climbout.

i) Another rule of thumb is: once you know that you can no longer land straight ahead on the runway, get your landing gear up. The retraction of the landing gear will affect the drag on your airplane. It will require a slight pitch up to maintain your climb speed.

Departure Procedures:

a) A downwind departure is one where you takeoff and maintain runway heading until 300 feet below traffic pattern altitude. You then fly the rectangular pattern around the field until you arrive at midfield, then exit the area with a 45 degree turn away from the field while continuing the climb.

b) A straight out departure is as it sounds. You simply climb on course, maintaining your alignment with the runway and depart the area.

c) The Tower or Departure Control would communicate to you any other type of departure. Unless otherwise directed, you would fly the runway heading until at least reaching traffic pattern altitude. At which time, you can perform a 90 degree, 45 degree, or a radial intercept departure. This will prevent you from accidentally flying into another airplane which has entered the traffic pattern from below.

Leveling off at an altitude from a climb:

a) If you wait until you're right at the altitude before pushing your nose over, then you will shoot right past it and get yelled at by Professor Calfior! A general rule of thumb is to lead your altitude by 10 percent of your rate of climb. But for simplicity's sake, always start to push your nose over gently at 100 feet prior to your desired cruise or level off altitude.

b) Now there's a trick to this leveling off. You are at climb airspeed, and as you lower your nose to slow down your climb rate, your airspeed will increase. As your airspeed increases, your nose wants to go back up! So while the airspeed is steadily increasing, until it stabilizes, you will need to scoot the nose down a little bit and a little bit and a little bit, in order to hold on to that target altitude. Notice this whenever you level off.

Controlling the Airplane:

When maneuvering the airplane, a recommended control sequence to follow in visual flight is:

a) **Visualize** the desired new flight path and airspeed.

b) **Select the attitude and the power required** to achieve the desired performance by moving the controls, and then verifying that the airplane has achieved the estimated attitude.

c) **Hold the attitude**, allowing the airplane to settle down into its new performance.

d) **Make small adjustments** to attitude and power until the actual performance equals the desired performance.

e) **Trim**. Heavy loads can be trimmed off earlier in the sequence to assist in control, if desired. But remember that the function of trim is to relieve control loads on the pilot, and not to change aircraft attitude.

Turns:

a) One thing you will notice immediately is that whenever you start a turn, the airplane will want to descend. This is because some of the vertical lift is now heading in the horizontal direction, so you need to give the required vertical lift a boost of energy! As you smoothly commence your turn, bring your nose up a thought! (That's how little you'll need at a standard rate turn)

b) Another gee-whiz feature about this simulator is that once you are established in your turn, the airplane has a tendency to want to slip deeper into the turn. So watch for that, because you want your airplane wing, on the turn indicator, to be pegged right on the "L" or "R" indicator. As it tries to deepen further, tap that wing in the opposite direction just a mite! Don't over control the plane in a rock and roll move throughout the turn!

c) When it comes to rolling out of a turn to a predetermined heading, the first few scenarios will help you by telling you what heading to begin your rollout on. On the average, it's anywhere from 7 to 12 degrees short of your heading mark. Later on, it's expected that you will acquire an eye for your roll rate and start the rollout on your own as to arrive right on your desired heading.

d) Now think about Part **(a)** up above. It's logical that as you start to roll your wings to the level position, all that extra nose up movement you've put in will want to make your airplane climb! So as you start that rollout, smoothly push your nose down a little in order to hold that altitude.

VOR Tracking on a radial:

Now we're getting into the instrument training side of VFR flying.

a) When you have intercepted your desired course, the CDI needle should be centered with either a "TO" or a "FROM" indication. If there were no winds to blow you off course, that needle would stay centered. But that generally does not happen, so something called tracking and bracketing is done.

b) Whenever you notice you're drifting off course, (that is, the CDI needle is moving from its center position), make a 20 degree correction in the direction that the needle is moving. Hold that 20 degree correction until you see that the needle is back to its centered position.

c) Now take 10 degrees out of your heading correction, and watch that needle. If it remains centered, your 10 degree crab angle is the correction you need to hold that desired radial. But if the needle starts moving now in the opposite direction, the 10 degrees is too much of a correction. So turn to the heading which parallels your radial and drift back to a centered needle.

d) When the needle centers, make a 5 degree correction in the original direction and that should keep your needle centered.

e) If the first 20 degrees of heading change does not force your CDI needle to head back towards the center, then put in another 20 degrees in the same direction. You're obviously in a strong crosswind. When the needle finally centers, take out 20 of those degrees and see how your needle reacts.

Reading the VOR CDI:

The VOR OBI has a needle which moves to the left or right of center, depending on whether you are left or right of your intended radial. There are four visible dots to the right and left with a small circle between them. The circle is covering the first dot which would be to the left and right of the center of the circle. Therefore, when the needle, called the CDI, is over the left edge of the circle, it is one dot to the left of center.

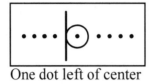

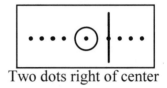

One dot left of center   Two dots right of center

When you are flying these scenarios, and a command tells you to turn to a specific heading when your NAV 1 or 2 CDI is two dots RIGHT of center, you must count the circle's edge as dot one.

Descents:

a) When beginning a descent, you will be reducing the power to a certain predesignated RPM setting. What is important to note is that more than a 1,000 feet per minute rate of descent is considered excessive. As a generalization, 400 to 700 feet per minute is a good average descent rate. The aircraft is well in control, and that is the primary safety consideration. When you start working in instrument meteorological conditions, instrument approaches are always geared to the 400 to 700 feet per minute descent rate. So it's a good habit pattern to build for controllability and safety.

b) If coming in for an approach to your destination, the level off from the descent may be such that you will keep your power setting at its reduced level, to help slow down for traffic pattern operations. If you are still in the en route portion of your flight, it would be wise to lead the level off by 10 to 20 percent of your rate of descent (depending on your descent rate) and to smoothly increase your power back to its cruise setting.

c) Always pay attention to your VSI (Vertical Speed Indicator) while in a descent. This is especially true when in the landing pattern, since a 400 feet per minute descent will quite accurately put you in the most ideal final approach position from the downwind leg. It's easy to lose that VSI from your scan and when you do remember to look, it's at 1500 feet per minute and the runway is looking quite flat up ahead! Make the VSI a constant reference of scan throughout any descent.

Traffic Pattern Entries:

a) The 45 degree entry to a right or left downwind is considered standard.

b) You could be directed to fly overhead the field and descend down into a right or left downwind, depending on your heading.

c) A straight in to a landing is possible where a long extended final approach accommodates the flow of arriving airplanes.

d) It's possible to be vectored to an immediate base leg at an extended distance.

e) Let us repeat once again the importance of realizing that, without any specific instructions from the tower or at an uncontrolled field, the standard traffic pattern is left hand, and a 45 degree entry will be what's expected. Other airplanes that are in the pattern will be expecting arrivals to come in via the 45 degree entry. *If you desire to enter differently, make sure that you communicate your position and anticipated approach method, so that others can look for you and exercise collision avoidance procedures by scanning for you where you say you are.*

Traffic Pattern Operations:

a) The scenarios in this companion utilize a variety of landing approaches. This was done to provide you with a multitude of landing experiences. But one thing to remember always: if an airport is uncontrolled, the basic landing pattern is left turns and the basic entry is a 45 degree entry. In the diagram which accompanies this section, for another varied view, we have shown you a **RIGHT** 45 degree entry.

b) To help you be directionally accurate, a right hand pattern is one where your turns are made to the right. Right to base leg - right to final. A left hand pattern is one where your turns are made to the left. Left to base leg - left to final.

c) When arriving via the 45 degree entry, be at your **Traffic Pattern Altitude** (which is usually 800 to 1000 feet above airport elevation) by at least two miles outside of the field. This is so that you can scan for aircraft that are already in the pattern at your horizon level eye view.

d) When there is a control tower on the field, **NEVER** go within five statute miles of the field unless you have called the Tower, and let them know you are coming in. That five statute mile radius area is called an Airport Traffic Area (ATA), and you never go in unannounced. By the way, if you are more than 3,000 feet above the airport elevation, then you are not in the Airport Traffic Area, so to fly overhead unannounced is okay!

e) When do you put your gear down? As a standard rule of thumb, your best bet will be whenever you are abeam midfield on your downwind leg. At this point, you should also take some of your power off so that you can slow down to an airspeed (**90 knots**) which will allow you to bring your flaps down to 10 degrees, or the **first notch**.

f) You are on the downwind leg when you are flying parallel to the runway you want to land on, about 1 mile wide of it, and 180 degrees in the opposite direction from your intended direction of landing. It's called downwind because it's where the wind is heading **DOWN** to!

g) When you are opposite your point of intended landing on the downwind, your airspeed should be low enough to permit you to lower your flaps. Take some more power off, and begin a descent at about a 400 feet per minute rate of descent. Stay on your downwind track until the approach end of the runway you want to land on is at your 5 o'clock position (**RIGHT DOWNWIND**) or 7 o'clock position (**LEFT DOWNWIND**).

h) When the runway threshold is at those o'clock positions, you should have descended approximately 200 to 300 feet below traffic pattern altitude. Begin your turn to the base leg, which brings you to the centerline of the extended runway, with you being 90 degrees from your final approach course. You will be approximately one mile from the threshold of the runway.

i) At about the 2 o'clock (**RIGHT PATTERN**) or 10 o'clock (**LEFT PATTERN**) orientation to the runway threshold, begin your turn to the final approach. At the completion of that turn, you should have descended approximately 400 to 500 feet below traffic pattern altitude.

j) Flaps are extended to the second notch (20 degrees) and third notch (30 degrees) at various points to help you acquire the best all around descent angle to the runway, and to configure the airplane so that the final approach is solidly stabilized.

k) From final inbound to touchdown, each scenario has a wealth of notes to help make the landing a totally inspired success. We do not agree with the saying "A safe landing is one you can walk away from!"

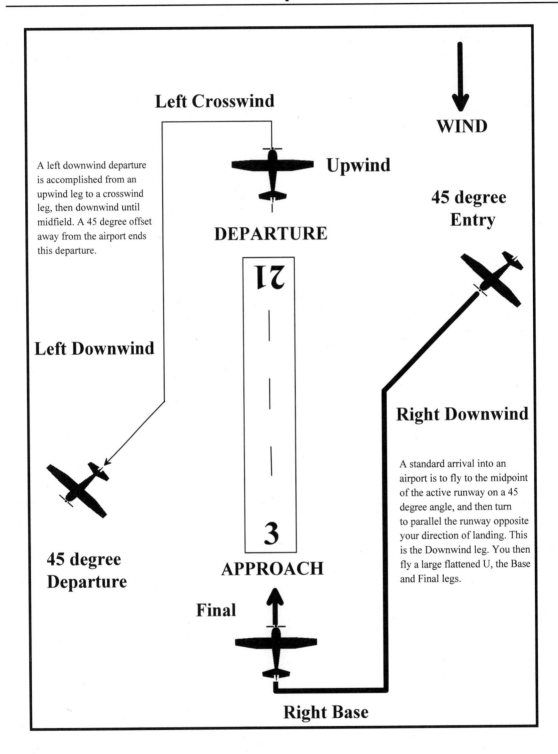

Left Crosswind

WIND

A left downwind departure is accomplished from an upwind leg to a crosswind leg, then downwind until midfield. A 45 degree offset away from the airport ends this departure.

Upwind

45 degree Entry

DEPARTURE

Left Downwind

Right Downwind

A standard arrival into an airport is to fly to the midpoint of the active runway on a 45 degree angle, and then turn to parallel the runway opposite your direction of landing. This is the Downwind leg. You then fly a large flattened U, the Base and Final legs.

45 degree Departure

APPROACH

Final

Right Base

✈ Flight Scenario One

Riverside to La Verne

(Los Angeles Area - estimated flying time 30 minutes)

Professor Miller here! Let me tell you about the first flight scenario. It departs Riverside Airport in the eastern portion of the Los Angeles Basin and arrives at La Verne Airport (Brackett Field) in the northern Los Angeles Basin. I will lead you through the initial setup phase of the flight simulator where you will set the aircraft type, winds, and position. I will show you how to save this setup so you may return to the Riverside Airport without going through the initial setup again. I will then turn you over to Professor Calfior, who will take you through the PREFLIGHT of "13MIKE" to set your instruments, TAXI, and perform a RUN UP of the engine prior to takeoff. He will instruct you in the TAKEOFF, CLIMB OUT, LEVEL OFF, COURSE CHANGES, DESCENT, APPROACH, and LANDING procedures that make up the bulk of this scenario. Remember to listen to what Professor Calfior has to say about flying techniques. He is trying to help you obtain the best possible score.

Let's look at our route of flight for this scenario. It has some interesting instrument procedures and an unusual approach.

FLIGHT PLAN -

The flight begins with a departure from runway 9 at Riverside Airport, with a climb out to 4500 feet. After departure you will be turning to a heading of 256 to intercept the POMONA 164 radial. You will be tracking inbound on the 164 radial, and performing a step descent to set up for a right downwind approach to La Verne's 26R (right) runway. Wow! A step down approach with a fly over of the runway. Sounds exciting! After filling out our flight plan in Appendix A, and calling the Flight Service Station (FSS) to file it, we need to turn to Appendix B, and locate the sectional map for Los Angeles. Find the Riverside and La Verne airports. Read the route of flight carefully and draw the route on the map. After you have finished drawing your route, answer the following questions. You may want to double check your route to be sure it is correct or you will lose these points.

** a) As you travel from East to West, what VOR do you pass?
_____ (15 pts)

** b) While heading West, what airport is just to your left?
_____ (15 pts)

** c) What VOR is just south of La Verne?
_____ (15 pts)

SETUP

Aircraft:

1) Choose "**Cessna Skylane RG**"

Weather:

1) Set Surface winds "**DEPTH**" to "**1000**"
2) Set Surface winds "**DIR**" to "**090**"
3) Set Surface winds "**SPEED**" to "**10**"

4) Set Level 1 "**TOPS**" to "**10000**"
5) Set Level 1 "**BASE**" to "**1000**"
6) Set Level 1 "**DIR**" to "**250**"
7) Set Level 1 "**SPEED**" to "**15**"

Aircraft Position:

1) "**NORTH**" to "**15289.5568**" -- [**N033° 57' 13.9161**]
2) "**EAST**" to "**6141.3893**" -- [**W117° 26' 39.9211**]
3) "**ALTITUDE**" to "**823**" -- [**0**]
4) "**HEADING**" to "**270**"

note: At this point you may wish to save this setup for future use.

PREFLIGHT

note: Set **ZOOM** to "1.0"
Set **TIME** to "10:00"

"Thank you Professor Miller! I'm Professor Calfior and it's time to find out what the local airport information is before we begin to taxi. It's called Automatic Terminal Information Service or ATIS for short, so go ahead and dial in the frequency 128.8 on our communication panel."

Instruments:

1) Tune **COM** to "**128.8**" (ATIS)

"RIVERSIDE MUNICIPAL, INFORMATION DELTA, 1645 ZULU WEATHER, SKY CLEAR, VISIBILITY 6, HAZE. TEMPERATURE 87, WIND 090 AT 10. ALTIMETER 30.01. LANDING AND DEPARTING RUNWAY 9. ADVISE ON INITIAL CONTACT YOU HAVE INFORMATION DELTA."

"All right! Winds are from the east, that's why runway 9 is the active runway. Let's go ahead and set up the instruments as we know we'll need them."

2) Set "**Altimeter**" and "**DG**"
3) Set **XPDR** to "**1200**" (VFR code)
4) Tune **NAV 1** to "**112.2**" (PDZ)
5) Set **NAV 1 OBS** to "**282**" in the upper window
6) Tune **NAV 2** to "**110.4**" (POM)
7) Set **NAV 2 OBS** to "**344**" in the upper window
8) Set the **DME** to "**NAV 1**" and "**DIST**"
9) Check **CARB HEAT** is "**OFF**"
10) Check **GEAR** "**DOWN**"
11) Turn **STROBE** "**ON**"
12) Check **LIGHTS** are "**OFF**"

"Good, good! Let's go ahead and switch to Riverside Ground Control frequency, 121.7, and get our clearance to taxi out of here."

13) Tune **COM** to "**121.7**" (Ground)

You:

"RIVERSIDE GROUND, THIS IS CESSNA 13MIKE AT THE TERMINAL, READY TO TAXI TO RUNWAY 9 WITH INFORMATION DELTA."

Riverside Ground:

"13MIKE, TAXI TO RUNWAY 9."

1

TAXI -

"Runway 9 is to our left, so taxi straight ahead to the touch down area for runway 9. When we get to the beginning of runway 9, turn left to face the runway, but hold short of the runway. We will do our runup here." See Figure 1.1

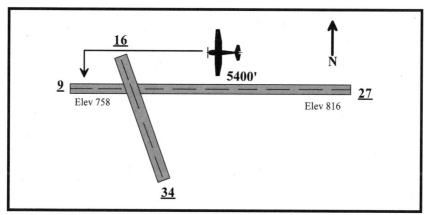

Figure 1.1.   Taxi to runway 9.

RUNUP -

"Outstanding job! Now before we takeoff, let's make sure that our engine is operating as it should, by checking its magnetos and finishing off with the pretake-off checklist."

           1) Set brake (hold down to prevent aircraft from moving)
           2) Advance power to about **"1700"** RPM
**   3) Select CARB HEAT **"ON"**, record RPM drop_____(5 pts)
           4) Select CARB HEAT **"OFF"**
**   5) Select **"LEFT"** Mag, record RPM drop_____(5 pts)
           6) Select **"BOTH"** Mags
**   7) Select **"RIGHT"** Mag, record RPM drop_____(5 pts)
           8) Select **"BOTH"** Mags

9) Reduce power to **idle**

10) Set **FLAPS** to **first notch** (10 degree takeoff configuration)

"Well, there are only two things left to do! Activate your VFR flight plan with Riverside Ground and then change over to Riverside Tower's frequency to get our clearance for takeoff. Go ahead!"

You:

"RIVERSIDE GROUND, 13MIKE WOULD LIKE TO ACTIVATE ITS VFR FLIGHT PLAN TO LA VERNE."

Riverside Ground:

"13MIKE, YOUR VFR FLIGHT PLAN IS ACTIVATED AT THIS TIME."

You:

"13MIKE."

11) Tune **COM** to **"121.0"** (Tower)

You:

"RIVERSIDE TOWER, CESSNA 13MIKE, READY FOR TAKEOFF RUNWAY 9."

Riverside Tower:

"13MIKE, YOU ARE CLEARED FOR TAKEOFF."

You:

"13MIKE CLEARED FOR TAKEOFF."

FLIGHT

1

Takeoff:

"Hey, what a deal! Okay, now check your flap settings, we've got plenty of fuel - full tanks, we're trimmed for takeoff, oil temperature and oil pressure are within limits. Good! Let's taxi onto runway 9, line up on the centerline, and let's hit the air!"

1) Record TIME _____
2) Release brakes and taxi onto runway 9
3) Advance power to **"FULL"**
4) Maintain centerline of runway
5) At **50 knots** airspeed lift nose wheel off runway
6) At **70 knots** ease back on the yoke to establish a 10 degree pitch up attitude
7) Maintain a climb **AIRSPEED** of **80 knots**
8) Raise **Gear** when there is no more runway to land on
9) At **"500"** feet above the ground raise the **FLAPS** to **"0"**
10) Reduce power to about **"2300"** RPM at **"1000"** feet above the ground (AGL)

"This should give you approximately an '800' feet per minute climb rate on your Vertical Speed Indicator (VSI). You're looking good there!"

Climb out:

1) Maintain runway heading and climb to **"2300"** feet
2) At **"2300"** feet start a climbing **RIGHT** turn

"All your turns should be STANDARD RATE. You make a STANDARD RATE turn by keeping the wings on the little airplane displayed on the TURN COORDINATOR aligned with the 'R' indicator."

3) Start to roll out when you see **"245"** in the DG window

    4) Maintain a heading of **"256"**

"Now you just keep that heading steady and keep in mind that winds can have a big effect on your actual ground track compared to what you have planned."

Level off:

    1) Begin to level off when the altimeter reads **"4400"** feet

    2) Maintain **"4500"** feet

    3) Reduce power to about **"2200"** **[2400]** RPM

"As you can tell, the intensity of a cross country flight is ever-present at takeoff, then it settles down to a lull for the en route portion. Then it hums into activity once again when coming in for the arrival, and into the landing. For instance, see how that NAV 2 CDI needle is now starting to move towards the center? Watch how quickly things begin to happen now!!!"

Course change:

    1) Watch your **NAV 2 CDI**, when the needle is one dot **LEFT** of center start your turn to a heading of **"344"** (standard rate)

    2) When your heading indicator reads **"335"** start to roll out

    3) After you have rolled out, press **"P"** to pause the simulation

**   4) Record your:

        NAV 1 DME DIST_____(25 pts)

        NAV 2 DME DIST_____(25 pts)

        ALTITUDE_____(20 pts)

        AIRSPEED_____(15 pts)

        GEAR_____(10 pts)

        FLAPS_____(10 pts)

        MAGS_____(10 pts)

        STROBE_____(10 pts)

        LIGHTS_____(10 pts)

    5) Press **"P"** to continue the simulation

6) Track inbound on the **"164"** radial (344 course) that your **NAV 2 OBI** is displaying

"To track inbound on a VOR radial, you keep the CDI needle centered making minor heading changes to compensate for winds."

Descent:

1) While tracking inbound on the **POMONA VOR 164** radial, descend and maintain **"2500"** feet

*"Now that we've commenced our descent, it's always a smart thing to get your destination's ATIS information, which by the way is on frequency **124.4**, and check that everything looks okay in this cockpit! Man, oh man, you are flying this cross country superbly! Keep up the good work!"*

2) Tune **COM** to **"124.4"** (La Verne ATIS)

"LA VERNE BRACKETT FIELD, INFORMATION GOLF, 1705 ZULU WEATHER, SKY CLEAR, VISIBILITY 8 WITH HAZE. TEMPERATURE 88, WIND 270 AT 8. ALTIMETER 29.97. LANDING RUNWAY 26 RIGHT, DEPARTING RUNWAY 26 LEFT. ADVISE ON INITIAL CONTACT YOU HAVE INFORMATION GOLF."

3) Set **ALTIMETER**, set **DG**, and check **FUEL**

*"Now, before we enter into La Verne Brackett Field's airport traffic area, which is a five statute mile radius when the tower is in operation, let Tower know that you're coming in and you have ATIS information GOLF. La Verne Tower frequency is **118.2**."*

4) Tune **COM** to **"118.2"** (La Verne Tower)

You:

>"LA VERNE TOWER, THIS IS CESSNA 13MIKE, ABOUT SIX MILES SOUTH OF THE FIELD, INBOUND FOR LANDING WITH GOLF."

La Verne Tower:

>"13MIKE, OVERFLY THE FIELD AT 2500 FEET AND TURN RIGHT DOWNWIND FOR LANDING ON RUNWAY 26 RIGHT. REPORT WHEN OVERHEAD THE FIELD."

You:

>"13MIKE, REPORT WHEN OVERHEAD THE FIELD."

** 5) Record the **NAV 2 DME DIST** when **NAV 1 CDI** needle centers _____ (25 pts)
6) At "**2500**" feet reduce power to about "**1600**" [**1900**] RPM

Approach:

"Hey, look there! See La Verne's parallel runways in front of you? You've been right on track and can now have some fun with this approach and landing!

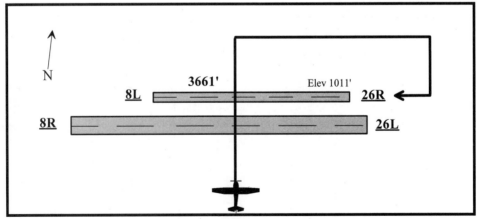

Figure 1.2.   90 degree entry to overfly runway 26 Right.

1) Fly over the runways at "**2500**" feet and turn **RIGHT** to enter a RIGHT DOWNWIND for runway 26R (right)

"This looks good! Give yourself enough distance from the runway before you start your turn to the downwind. You can judge when you've got enough distance by looking out your right rear quarter window. Go on and tell Tower that you're overhead the field."

** *"By the way, what would your downwind course be when parallel to runway 26R?"* _____ (10 pts)

You:

> "LA VERNE TOWER, 13MIKE IS OVERHEAD AT THIS TIME."

La Verne Tower:

> "13MIKE, YOU MAY DESCEND TO TRAFFIC PATTERN ALTITUDE. YOU'RE CLEARED FOR LANDING ON RUNWAY 26 RIGHT."

You:

> "LA VERNE TOWER, 13MIKE IS CLEARED TO LAND."

** *"Hey! What is that traffic pattern altitude anyway?"* _____ (15 pts)

** 2) When established on the DOWNWIND leg of the approach, record the heading displayed on your DG _____ (20 pts)

3) Select **GEAR "DOWN"**

"You should be able to see the runway out your right window. If you cannot see the runway, you may be too close."

"If you're too close, what action could you take to get into proper position of this right downwind? Why don't you simply jog to the left for a 30 degree offset, and after 10 seconds, come on back to your downwind heading."

4) **CARB HEAT "ON"**

5) Reduce throttle to about **"1400" [1700]** RPM (this is the beginning of your approach descent)

6) When you have slowed to **90** knots set **FLAPS** to **first notch** (10 degrees)

7) Try and maintain a **400** ft per minute descent on your Vertical Speed Indicator (VSI)

"Keep in mind that in the landing phase, always adjust height with power, and airspeed with pitch. It'll make approach and landings so much simpler for you."

8) When the end of the runway is at your 5 o'clock position, turn **RIGHT "90"** degrees to establish your **BASE** leg of the approach. (heading of 170 degrees)

"See how that runway looks off to your right now? You're heading back toward the runway very nicely. Get ready to turn on final soon!"

9) Set **FLAPS** to **second notch** (20 degrees)

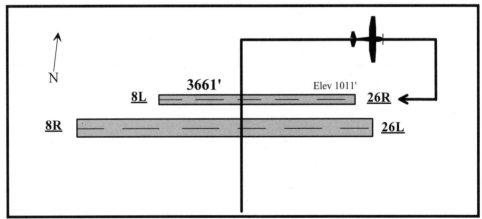

Figure 1.3. Downwind turning Right Base for runway 26 Right.

10) Press "**P**" to pause the simulation

** 11) Record your:

AIRSPEED_____(25 pts)
RPM_____(25 pts)
VSI_____(20 pts)
ALTITUDE_____(20 pts)
HEADING_____(15 pts)
CARB HEAT_____(10 pts)

12) Press "**P**" to continue the simulation

13) When runway 26 R (right) is at your 2 o'clock position, start a "**90**" degree **RIGHT** turn to establish your **FINAL** leg of the approach.

"Just keep in mind that if you're not lined up with runway 26 R (right), then make slight heading adjustments to compensate for winds, overshoots, or undershoots. At all costs, keep those corrections small!"

14) When established on the **FINAL** leg, set **FLAPS** to **third notch** (30 degrees)

15) Airspeed should be **70 knots**

"Again, let me remind you that you always adjust height with power, and airspeed with pitch. It sure makes life easier on final approach, that's for sure!"

16) When the **ALTIMETER** displays "**1300**" feet, press "**P**" to pause the simulation

** 17) Record your:

AIRSPEED_____(25 pts)
VSI_____(25 pts)
HEADING_____(20 pts)
RPM_____(25 pts)
FLAPS_____(15 pts)

18) Press "**P**" to continue the simulation

19) When you are 10 to 20 feet off the runway, reduce power to about "**1000**" RPM, and slowly start to pitch the nose of the aircraft up to reduce the speed of your descent and establish a touchdown attitude

*"WATCH YOUR **AIRSPEED**! Be careful not to stall the aircraft. Do not let your airspeed drop below **60 knots,** or else you'll fall out of the sky. We're not ready for that maneuver yet!"*

20) When you are five feet off the runway, hold the nose of the aircraft up and allow the airspeed to **SLOWLY** bleed off. Your aircraft will <u>settle</u> onto the runway while you follow the centerline.

"Don't be impatient! Let the aircraft <u>settle</u> onto the runway slowly. There's lots of runway in front of you, so there's no hurry."

21) After touchdown reduce power to **600 RPM**
22) Apply the brakes, turn left, and taxi off the active runway
23) When aircraft has stopped, set **CARB HEAT** to "OFF"
24) Set **FLAPS** to "0"

*"Nice job! The flight is not over, until the engine stops where we want it to stop! So let's switch to Ground Control on **125.0** and get our taxi clearance. Let's wait to close your flight plan when you get inside the terminal, and then give Flight Service Station a call on the telephone."*

25) Tune **COM** to "125.0" (Ground)

You:

"LA VERNE GROUND, CESSNA 13MIKE IS DOWN AND CLEAR OF RUNWAY 26 RIGHT FOR TAXI TO THE TERMINAL."

La Verne Ground:

"13MIKE, CLEARED TO TAXI TO THE TERMINAL."

**   26) Record the **TIME** _____ (5 pts)

TOTAL POINTS POSSIBLE FOR THIS FLIGHT IS **495**

✈ Flight Scenario Two

La Verne to Santa Monica

(Los Angeles Area - estimated flying time 30 minutes)

Professor Miller here again! How did you like that approach into La Verne? I'll bet it kept you busy. Well, the next flight has a few interesting surprises. It departs La Verne Airport and proceeds west to Santa Monica Airport. You need to watch out for the Los Angeles TCA. Well, let's get started. If you are continuing on with Professor Calfior in "13MIKE", you may skip the "SETUP" section and proceed to the section labeled "PREFLIGHT". If this is your first flight with "13MIKE", let me tell you how we do the setup. I will lead you through the initial setup phase of the flight simulator where you will set the aircraft type, winds, and position. I will show you how to save this setup so you may return to the La Verne Airport without going through the initial setup again. I will then turn you over to Professor Calfior, who will take you through the PREFLIGHT of "13MIKE" to set your instruments, TAXI, and perform a RUN UP of the engine prior to takeoff. He will instruct you in the TAKEOFF, CLIMB OUT, LEVEL OFF, COURSE CHANGES, DESCENT, APPROACH, and LANDING procedures that make up the bulk of this scenario. Again I would like to remind you to listen to what Professor Calfior has to say about flying techniques. He is trying to help you obtain the best possible score.

Our route of flight for this scenario has some interesting instrument procedures, you will need to keep sharp.

FLIGHT PLAN -

The procedures begin with a departure from runway 26L (left) at La Verne Airport and a climb out to 4000 feet. After departure you will be turning to a heading of 130 degrees to intercept the POMONA 164 radial. You will fly outbound on the POMONA 164 radial to intercept the PARADISE 276 radial. A right turn to a heading of 276 will allow you to track outbound on the PARADISE radial. You will change altitude to 4500, after avoiding the Los Angeles TCA. Upon reaching the halfway point between the PARADISE and VAN NUYS VORs, you will track inbound on the VAN NUYS 096 radial. This will set you up to intercept the 032 radial from the SANTA MONICA VOR and track inbound. You will start your descent to 2600 feet, which will begin your straight in approach to Santa Monica airport's runway 21. This course parallels a TCA wall and you must take care not to wander off course or you may end up busting the TCA. I think you're going to be busy on this one. After filling out our flight plan in Appendix A, and calling the Flight Service Station (FSS) to file it, we need to turn to Appendix B and locate the sectional map for Los Angeles. Find La Verne and Santa Monica airports. Draw the above route carefully on the map. Answer these questions.

**   a) What is the altitude of the floor of the TCA where you fly under it?
_____(15 pts)

**   b) What famous horse race track is just North of your route?
_____(15 pts)

**   c) What is the name of the airport you fly over?
_____(15 pts)

SETUP

Aircraft:
1) Choose **"Cessna Skylane RG"**

Weather:
1) Set Surface winds **"DEPTH"** to **"1000"**

2) Set Surface winds "**DIR**" to "**270**"
3) Set Surface winds "**SPEED**" to "**10**"
4) Set Level 1 "**TOPS**" to "**10000**"
5) Set Level 1 "**BASE**" to "**1000**"
6) Set Level 1 "**DIR**" to "**250**"
7) Set Level 1 "**SPEED**" to "**15**"

Aircraft Position:

1) "**NORTH**" to "**15377.6121**" -- [N034° 05' 30.0594]
2) "**EAST**" to "**6037.8823**" -- [W117° 46' 45.5292]
3) "**ALTITUDE**" to "**1016**" -- [0]
4) "**HEADING**" to "**170**"

note: At this point you may wish to save this setup for future use.

PREFLIGHT

note: Set **ZOOM** to "**1.0**"
Set **TIME** to "**11:05**"

"Yeah! Isn't Professor Miller a cool setter-upper?! I'm Professor Calfior for those of you who are new, or to those of you who have forgotten me already! I'll be flying with you in the right seat for this flight, and to begin this cross country properly, let's get our ATIS information. Let me see, the frequency is - oh yeah, 124.4! Dial it into the communication panel."

Instruments:

1) Tune **COM** to "**124.4**" (ATIS)

"LA VERNE BRACKETT FIELD, INFORMATION SIERRA, 1800 ZULU WEATHER, SKY CLEAR, VISIBILITY FIVE IN HAZE. TEMPERATURE 93, WIND 270 AT 10. ALTIMETER 29.96. CAUTION FOR MOWERS OPERATING NEAR THE APPROACH END OF RUNWAYS 26 RIGHT AND 26 LEFT. ALL AIRCRAFT DEPARTURES ARE ON RUNWAY 26 LEFT - ALL ARRIVALS LANDING ON RUNWAY 26 RIGHT. ADVISE ON INITIAL CONTACT YOU HAVE INFORMATION SIERRA."

"They don't get any more exciting than that, do they?!! Mowers! They're probably spies critiquing all the landings to the airport general manager! Well anyway, runway 26L is where we need to go. Let's set up the instruments as we need them before we think about taxiing."

2) Set **"Altimeter"** and **"DG"**
3) Set **XPDR** to **"1200"** (VFR code)
4) Tune **NAV 1** to **"110.4"** (POM)
5) Set **NAV 1 OBS** to **"164"** in the upper window
6) Tune **NAV 2** to **"112.2"** (PDZ)
7) Set **NAV 2 OBS** to **"276"** in the upper window
8) Set the **DME** to **"NAV 1"** and **"DIST"**
9) Check **CARB HEAT** is **"OFF"**
10) Check **GEAR "DOWN"**
11) Turn **STROBE "ON"**
12) Check **LIGHTS** are **"OFF"**

*"Ready to taxi? Now double check one more time that you've got your cockpit in order, and then switch to La Verne's Ground Control frequency, **125.0**, and get a clearance to taxi to Santa Monica - I mean to 26L so we can get to Santa Monica!"*

13) Tune **COM** to **"125.0"** (Ground)

You:

> **"LA VERNE GROUND, THIS IS CESSNA 13MIKE AT THE RAMP, READY TO TAXI TO RUNWAY 26 LEFT WITH INFORMATION SIERRA."**

La Verne Ground:

> **"13MIKE, TAXI TO RUNWAY 26 LEFT. USE CAUTION FOR MOWERS IN THE VICINITY."**

You:

> **"13MIKE."**

2

TAXI -

> *"You are facing runway 26L (left). Make a left turn and taxi to the beginning of the touchdown area for runway 26L. When you get to the departure end of 26L, turn right and hold short of the runway. We will go through our runup here."* See Figure 2.1.

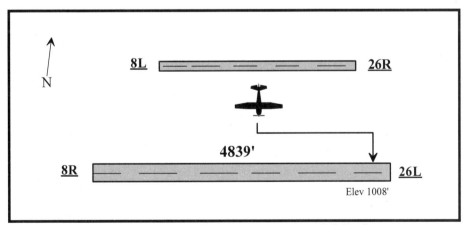

Figure 2.1.   Taxi to runway 26 Left.

RUNUP -

1) Set brake (hold down to prevent aircraft from moving)
2) Advance power to about **"1800"** RPM
** 3) Select CARB HEAT **"ON"**, record RPM drop_____(5 pts)
4) Select CARB HEAT **"OFF"**
** 5) Select **"LEFT"** Mag, record RPM drop_____(5 pts)
6) Select **"BOTH"** Mags
** 7) Select **"RIGHT"** Mag, record RPM drop_____(5 pts)
8) Select **"BOTH"** Mags
9) Reduce power to **idle**
10) Set **FLAPS** to **first notch** (10 degrees takeoff configuration)

"Yup, you're certainly right! Now that you've completed your pretake-off checklist, the next step is to activate your flight plan."

You:

"LA VERNE GROUND, 13MIKE WOULD LIKE TO ACTIVATE ITS VFR FLIGHT PLAN TO SANTA MONICA AT THIS TIME."

La Verne Ground:

"13MIKE, YOUR VFR FLIGHT PLAN IS ACTIVATED. HAVE A NICE FLIGHT."

You:

"13MIKE, GOOD DAY!"

"There's no line of airplanes in front of us, and you look ready to go - you are, aren't you? Then get us on Tower frequency, 118.2, and get our clearance for takeoff."

11) Tune **COM** to **"118.2"** (La Verne Tower)

You:

"LA VERNE TOWER, CESSNA 13MIKE, READY FOR DEPARTURE RUNWAY 26 LEFT."

La Verne Tower:

"13MIKE, YOU ARE CLEARED FOR TAKEOFF."

You:

"13MIKE CLEARED FOR TAKEOFF."

FLIGHT

Takeoff:

"Now, as you're moving and getting lined up on the centerline of 26R, check your flap settings, the fuel gauges indicate 'FULL', check your trim setting - it's in the takeoff position, good - and oil temperature and pressure both are within limits. Let's go!"

1) Record TIME _____
2) Release brakes and taxi onto runway 26L
3) Advance power to **"FULL"**
4) Maintain centerline of runway
5) At **50 knots** airspeed lift nose wheel off runway
6) At **70 knots** ease back on the yoke to establish a 10 degree pitch up attitude
7) Maintain a climb **AIRSPEED** of **80 knots**
8) Raise **Gear** when there is no more runway to land on
9) At **"500"** feet above the ground raise the **FLAPS** to **"0"**
10) Reduce power to about **"2300"** RPM at **"1000"** feet above the ground (AGL)

*"This should give you approximately an **'800'** feet per minute climb rate on your Vertical Speed Indicator (VSI). Now remember, if your VSI goes higher or lower, simply adjust with your nose."*

Climb out:

1) Maintain runway heading and climb to **"2400"** feet
2) At **"2400"** feet start a climbing **LEFT** turn

"All your turns should be STANDARD RATE. You make a STANDARD RATE turn by keeping the wings on the little airplane displayed on the TURN COORDINATOR aligned with the 'L' indicator."

3) Start to roll out when you see **"140"** in the DG window
4) Maintain a heading of **"130"**

"Now winds have a tendency to goof up your planned ground track which you've drawn quite nicely on your VFR sectional. So look for landmarks along the way, but be figuring out how those winds might be taking you slightly off track also."

5) Watch your **NAV 1 CDI**, when the needle is three dots **LEFT** of center, start your **RIGHT** turn to a heading of **"164"**
6) Track outbound on the **POMONA VOR 164** radial

"WOW! You lead that turn so beautifully, the CDI needle is pegged right down the middle! If the needle even thinks about moving, make minor heading changes to compensate for winds which are causing the needle to move."

Level off:

1) Begin to level off when the altimeter reads **"3900"** feet
2) Maintain **"4000"** feet
3) Reduce power to about **"2200"** **[2400]** RPM

"You know, if I didn't know any better, I'd say this airplane is flying on autopilot! You are so smooth in controlling this airplane! Now, let's look at your next step based upon the preflight planning you've accomplished for this flight."

Course change #1:

1) Watch your **NAV 2 CDI**, when the needle is one dot **LEFT** of center, start your **RIGHT** turn to a heading of "**276**"

2) When your heading indicator reads "**265**" start to roll out

3) After you have rolled out, press "**P**" to pause the simulation

** 4) Record your:

NAV 1 DME DIST_____(25 pts)
ALTITUDE_____(25 pts)
AIRSPEED_____(20 pts)
VSI_____(15 pts)
GEAR_____(10 pts)
FLAPS_____(10 pts)
MAGS _____(10 pts)
STROBE_____(5 pts)
LIGHTS_____(5 pts)

5) Press "**P**" to continue the simulation

6) Track outbound on the **PARADISE VOR 276** radial that your **NAV 2 OBI** is displaying

7) Switch **DME** to "**NAV 2**"

"If you constantly drift to the right, you need to make a wind correction for the heading you're on. Try and offset to the left about 20 degrees. An exact offset can be computed. We won't have the time to go into it now, but remind me to show you the Wind Correction section in your flight manual when we get down."

Altitude change:

1) When the **DME** on **NAV 2** reads "**29.0**", press "**P**" to pause the simulation

** 2) Record your:

      ALTITUDE_____(20 pts)

      AIRSPEED_____(20 pts)

      VSI_____(20 pts)

      HEADING_____(20 pts)

3) Press **"P"** to continue the simulation

4) Tune **NAV 1** to **"113.1"** and set radial **"276"** in the upper window

5) Track inbound on the **VAN NUYS VOR "096"** radial (course 276) that your **NAV 1 OBI** is displaying

6) Switch **DME** to **"NAV 1"**

"Let's go ahead and climb up to '4500' feet now since, as you notice on this sectional, we're clear of the Los Angeles TCA segment whose floor was 4000 feet."

7) Climb and maintain **"4500"** feet

Course change #2:

1) Tune your **NAV 2** to **"110.8"** and set radial **"212"** in the upper window

2) When the **NAV 2 CDI** needle is one dot **RIGHT** of center, start your **LEFT** turn to a heading of **"212"**

3) When your heading indicator reads **"225"**, start to roll out

4) After you have rolled out, press **"P"** to pause the simulation

** 5) Record your:

      NAV 1 DME DIST_____(25 pts)

      NAV 2 DME DIST_____(25 pts)

      ALTITUDE_____(20 pts)

      AIRSPEED_____(20 pts)

      VSI_____(15 pts)

6) Press **"P"** to continue the simulation

7) Track inbound on the **SANTA MONICA VOR "032"** radial (course 212) that your **NAV 2 OBI** is displaying

8) Switch **DME** to **"NAV 2"**

Descent:

1) While tracking inbound on the SANTA MONICA **"032"** radial, descend and maintain **"2600"** feet

*"As we are approaching Santa Monica's airport traffic area, let's get our ATIS information off of frequency **119.15**. Now look sharp on this specific tracking inbound, because off to your left is that TCA wall whose floor is 2500 feet. We certainly don't need any TCA violation, do we?"*

2) Tune **COM** to **"119.15"** (Santa Monica ATIS)

"SANTA MONICA MUNICIPAL, INFORMATION FOXTROT, 1830 ZULU WEATHER, SKY CLEAR, VISIBILITY SEVEN, TEMPERATURE 91, WIND 260 AT 9. ALTIMETER 29.95. LANDING AND DEPARTING RUNWAY 21. ADVISE ON INITIAL CONTACT YOU HAVE INFORMATION FOXTROT."

3) Set **ALTIMETER**, set **DG**, and check **FUEL**

"Hey! Dodger Stadium! Griffith Park Observatory! Hollywood Bowl! WOW! And to think most people don't even see this kind of view their entire life like we do! Makes you glad to be a pilot, doesn't it? Okay, no rush, but keep an eye on your DME into Santa Monica because you'll need to call Tower before reaching 5.0. The airport traffic area, remember?"

4) When the **NAV 2 DME DIST** reads **"6.7"**, descend to **"1200"** feet

*"Now go ahead and call Tower on **120.1**. It'd sure be nice to get that straight in we've planned for!"*

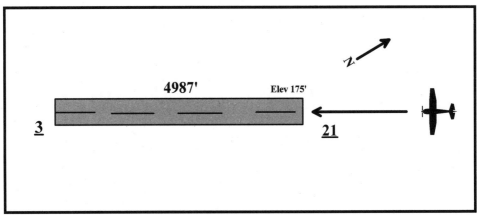

Figure 2.2.   Straight in approach to Santa Monica Airport

Approach:

"By the way, you can see that this is like a long "FINAL" leg of the approach, which is why it's called a straight in approach.   Look! There's Santa Monica's runway 21!" See Figure 2.2

1) Tune **COM** to "**120.1**" (Santa Monica Tower)

You:

"SANTA MONICA TOWER, THIS IS CESSNA 13MIKE, ABOUT SIX MILES NORTHEAST OF THE FIELD. REQUEST A STRAIGHT IN APPROACH TO RUNWAY 21 WITH FOXTROT."

Santa Monica Tower:

"13MIKE, STRAIGHT IN APPROACH IS APPROVED FOR LANDING ON RUNWAY 21. REPORT WHEN ON A FOUR MILE FINAL."

You:

> **"13MIKE, WILL REPORT A FOUR MILE FINAL."**
>
> 2) Select **GEAR "DOWN"**
> 3) **CARB HEAT "ON"**
> 4) When **NAV 2 DME DIST** reads "**5.0**", give four mile report

You:

> **"SANTA MONICA TOWER, 13MIKE IS ON A FOUR MILE FINAL AT THIS TIME."**

Santa Monica Tower:

> **"13MIKE, YOU ARE CLEARED TO LAND. YOUR TRAFFIC IS ON SHORT FINAL FOR A TOUCH AND GO."**

You:

> **"13MIKE CLEARED FOR LANDING. TRAFFIC IN SIGHT."**
>
> 5) Reduce power to about "**1400**" **[1700]** RPM (this is the beginning of your approach descent)
>
> 6) When you have slowed to **90 knots,** set **FLAPS** to **first notch** (10 degrees)
>
> 7) Try and maintain a **400** ft per minute descent on your Vertical Speed Indicator (VSI)

"Once again, as I've stated previously, always adjust height with power and airspeed with pitch in the landing phase. You're looking great attitude wise - memorize that picture of the approach end of the runway in relationship to your windscreen. That's what you always want. Don't let that picture shift other than getting bigger as you get closer."

> 8) When the **NAV 2 DME** reads "**3.0**", set **FLAPS** to **second notch** (20 degrees)

"Maintain the same runway aspect as you continue your descent. Don't let the runway rise or fall from its position in the windscreen. Look for that window about one mile out, and 500 feet above the ground, as you turn onto final."

9) When the **ALTIMETER** displays "**500**" feet, set **FLAPS** to **third notch** (30 degrees)

10) Airspeed should be **70 knots**

11) Press "**P**" to pause the simulation

** 12) Record your:

AIRSPEED_____(25 pts)
VSI_____(25 pts)
HEADING_____(20 pts)
RPM_____(15 pts)
FLAPS_____(15 pts)

13) Press "**P**" to continue the simulation

14) When you are 10 to 20 feet off the runway, reduce power to about "**1000**" RPM and start to slowly pitch the nose of the aircraft up to slow your descent, and establish a touchdown attitude

"WATCH YOUR AIRSPEED! Be careful not to stall the aircraft. Synchronize that power reduction and nose movement like a ballet move - nice and gentle. Don't let your airspeed drop below 60 knots."

15) When you are 5 feet off the runway, hold the nose of the aircraft up and allow the airspeed to **SLOWLY** bleed off. Your aircraft will **settle** onto the runway while you follow the centerline

*"Do not be impatient, let the aircraft **settle** onto the runway slowly. With almost 5000 feet of runway in front of you, the wheels don't have to plant themselves right on the numbers!"*

16) After touchdown reduce power to **600 RPM**

17) Apply the brakes

18) Turn left and taxi off the active runway

19) When the aircraft has stopped, set **CARB HEAT** to "OFF"

20) Set **FLAPS** to "0"

"All right, you flying Lindbergh, you! I'm quite proud of the way you handled this flight, especially with the L.A. shucks and jives that were involved! Now, switch to Ground Control on 121.9 and get our taxi clearance. Close your VFR flight plan while you're with them."

21) Tune **COM** to "121.9" (Santa Monica Ground)

You:

"SANTA MONICA GROUND, CESSNA 13MIKE IS DOWN AND CLEAR OF RUNWAY 21 FOR TAXI TO THE TERMINAL. I'D ALSO LIKE TO CLOSE MY VFR FLIGHT PLAN NOW."

Santa Monica Ground:

"13MIKE, YOUR VFR FLIGHT PLAN IS CLOSED, TAXI TO THE TERMINAL."

** 22) Record the **TIME**_____(5 pts)

TOTAL POINTS POSSIBLE FOR THIS FLIGHT IS ___475___

2

 # Flight Scenario Three

Santa Monica to Torrance

3

(Los Angeles Area - estimated flying time 30 minutes)

I believe you are fairly proficient at tracking a VOR radial by now. You probably had your head inside the cockpit more than outside on that last flight. Hi, this is Professor Miller again! You are half way through this four part flight. The next scenario is short on distance but long on communications. Flying through the Los Angeles TCA Corridor requires a sharp eye, concentration, and good communication skills. If you are continuing on with Professor Calfior in "13MIKE", you may skip the "SETUP" section and proceed to "PREFLIGHT". If this is your first flight with "13MIKE", let me tell you how we do the setup. I will lead you through the initial setup phase of the flight simulator where you will set the aircraft type, winds, and position. I will show you how to save this setup, so you may return to the Santa Monica Airport without going through the initial setup steps. I will then turn you over to Professor Calfior, who will take you through the PREFLIGHT of "13MIKE" to set your instruments, TAXI, and perform a RUN UP of the engine prior to takeoff. He will instruct you in the TAKEOFF, CLIMB OUT, LEVEL OFF, COURSE CHANGES, DESCENT, APPROACH, and LANDING procedures that make up the bulk of this scenario. Listen to what Professor Calfior has to say about flying techniques. He is trying to help you obtain the best possible score.

FLIGHT PLAN -

We depart from runway 21 at Santa Monica Airport with a climb out to 3500 feet. You will perform a standard right downwind departure. This will include a left 45 degree departure from the pattern. You will intercept the 140 radial from the VAN NUYS VOR and track outbound through the LAX TCA corridor. You will need to obtain permission from LA Approach Control to enter the corridor. After negotiating the corridor, you will setup for a 45 degree pattern entry, for runway 29R at Torrance. You will fly a normal, right downwind approach pattern to land at Torrance Airport. You are surrounded by the TCA, so take care not to wander off course or you may end up busting the TCA. You're going to be busy on this one. After filling out our flight plan in Appendix A, and calling the Flight Service Station (FSS) to file it, we need to turn to Appendix B and locate the sectional map for Los Angeles. Find Santa Monica and Torrance airports. Draw the above route on the map. Now answer these questions.

** a) What airport is to your left as you leave the LAX TCA Corridor?
_____(15 pts)

** b) How many runways does Los Angeles International have?
_____(15 pts)

** c) What is the height of the floor of the TCA at Santa Monica?
_____(15 pts)

SETUP

Aircraft:
1) Choose **"Cessna Skylane RG"**

Weather:
1) Set Surface winds **"DEPTH"** to **"1000"**
2) Set Surface winds **"DIR"** to **"270"**

3) Set Surface winds "**SPEED**" to "**10**"
4) Set Level 1 "**TOPS**" to "**10000**"
5) Set Level 1 "**BASE**" to "**1000**"
6) Set Level 1 "**DIR**" to "**250**"
7) Set Level 1 "**SPEED**" to "**15**"

Aircraft Position:

1) "**NORTH**" to "**15402.4744**" -- [N034° 00' 56.7211]
2) "**EAST**" to "**5799.4993**" -- [W118° 26' 59.2341]
3) "**ALTITUDE**" to "**180**" -- [0]
4) "**HEADING**" to "**120**"

note: At this point you may wish to save this setup for future use.

PREFLIGHT

note: Set **ZOOM** to "**1.0**"
Set **TIME** to "**12:30**"

"We could almost make believe we're a courier service dropping packages and parcels off from airport to airport, the way we've been touring the LA area! Again, thank you Professor Miller for your outstanding efficiency. I'm Professor Calfior and am I ever looking forward to this special puddle jump into the Los Angeles TCA corridor. Get your ATIS information on 119.15. Nah! Not your nav panel - your comm panel!"

Instruments:

1) Tune **COM** to "**119.15**" (ATIS)

"SANTA MONICA MUNICIPAL, INFORMATION CHARLIE, 1900 ZULU WEATHER, SKY CLEAR, VISIBILITY NINE. TEMPERATURE 89, WIND 270 AT 10. ALTIMETER 29.93. LANDING AND DEPARTING RUNWAY 21. ADVISE ON INITIAL CONTACT YOU HAVE INFORMATION CHARLIE."

"Sometimes in the early morning hours, ATIS will give you a dew point temperature because of its closeness to the actual temperature, which in turn brings fog. So we've landed on 21, and we now will takeoff on 21. It's getting pretty personal and familiar, isn't it? You go ahead and set up the instrument panel while I open this door and get my seat belt unwedged!"

2) Set "**Altimeter**"
3) Set "**DG**"
4) Set **XPDR** to "**1200**" (VFR code)
5) Tune **NAV 1** to "**113.1**" (VNY)
6) Set **NAV 1 OBS** to "**140**" in the upper window
7) Tune **NAV 2** to "**113.6**" (LAX)
8) Set **NAV 2 OBS** to "**010**" in the upper window
9) Set the **DME** to "**NAV 1**" and "**DIST**"
10) Check **CARB HEAT** is "**OFF**"
11) Check **GEAR** "**DOWN**"
12) Turn **STROBE** "**ON**"
13) Check **LIGHTS** are "**OFF**"

*"Once I swore the airplane was coming apart in the air, when this loud thumping noise kept on occurring. Then I realized that a portion of the seat belt strap had gotten caught outside when the door was shut, and the wind was whipping it all over tarnation! Well, I'm sure Ground is chomping at the bit to hear from us, so let's talk to them on **121.9**, shall we?!"*

14) Tune **COM** to "**121.9**" (Ground)

You:

> **"SANTA MONICA GROUND, THIS IS CESSNA 13MIKE AT THE TERMINAL, READY TO TAXI TO RUNWAY 21 WITH INFORMATION CHARLIE."**

Santa Monica Ground:

> **"13MIKE, TAXI TO RUNWAY 21 FOLLOWING THE BEECHCRAFT BONANZA PASSING YOU FROM THE RIGHT."**

You:

> **"13MIKE."**

TAXI -

> *"You are facing the taxiway with the runway to your back. Okay, there goes that Bonanza! Make a left 90 degree turn and taxi down to the runup area near the beginning of the threshold area of runway 21. Face the aircraft toward the runway, but not on the runway to perform your runup."* See Figure 3.1.

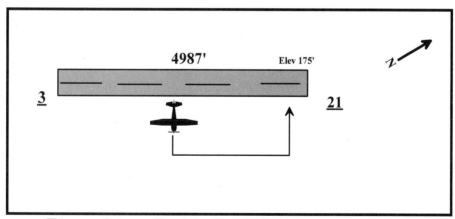

Figure 3.1.   Taxi to Santa Monica's runway 21.

RUN UP -

       1) Set brake (hold down to prevent aircraft from moving)

       2) Advance power to about "**1900**" RPM

**   3) Select CARB HEAT "**ON**", record RPM drop_____(5 pts)

       4) Select CARB HEAT "**OFF**"

**   5) Select "**LEFT**" Mag, record RPM drop_____(5 pts)

       6) Select "**BOTH**" Mags

**   7) Select "**RIGHT**" Mag, record RPM drop_____(5 pts)

       8) Select "**BOTH**" Mags

       9) Reduce power to **idle**

      10) Set **FLAPS** to **first notch** (10 degrees takeoff configuration)

"I've taken the liberty to scan over your flight plan and it looks very professional, neat, and well organized. Go ahead and activate your flight plan before we switch over to Tower."

You:

    "SANTA MONICA GROUND, 13MIKE WOULD LIKE TO ACTIVATE ITS VFR FLIGHT PLAN TO TORRANCE NOW."

Santa Monica Ground:

    "13MIKE, YOUR VFR FLIGHT PLAN IS ACTIVATED. ENJOY YOUR FLIGHT."

You:

    "13MIKE. THANKS FOR YOUR HELP."

*"If you feel comfortable and ready to go, have at it! Wait, wait!!! Get your clearance from Tower on **120.1**! I know you're excited, but you've got to play this 'Mother, may I' game first!"*

      11) Tune **COM** to "**120.1**" (Tower)

You:

    "SANTA MONICA TOWER, CESSNA 13MIKE, READY ON RUNWAY 21 FOR RIGHT DOWNWIND DEPARTURE."

Santa Monica Tower:

> **"13MIKE, YOU ARE CLEARED FOR TAKEOFF, RIGHT DOWNWIND DEPARTURE APPROVED."**

You:

> **"13MIKE IS CLEARED FOR TAKEOFF."**

FLIGHT

Takeoff:

"Okay! Line up real pretty on the centerline of 21, that's right - check your flaps, they're at 10 degrees, full fuel - good, trimmed for takeoff, and oil temperature and pressure both are within limits. Ready when you are!"

1) Record TIME _____
2) Release brakes and taxi onto runway 21
3) Advance power to "**FULL**"
4) Maintain centerline of runway
5) At **50 knots** airspeed lift nose wheel off runway
6) At **70 knots** ease back on the yoke to establish a 10 degree pitch up attitude
7) Maintain a climb **AIRSPEED** of **80 knots**
8) Raise **Gear** when there is no more runway to land on
9) At "**500**" feet above the ground raise the **FLAPS** to "**0**"
10) At "**700**" feet above the ground (which equates to the required 300 feet below traffic pattern altitude) turn **RIGHT 90** degrees to the **CROSSWIND** leg
11) When wings are level, begin your **RIGHT 90** degree turn to the **DOWNWIND** leg

"Now just keep tracking with that runway off your right side. It's just like a normal traffic pattern, but you're simply not leveling off at traffic pattern altitude. Feels funny to keep climbing, doesn't it?"

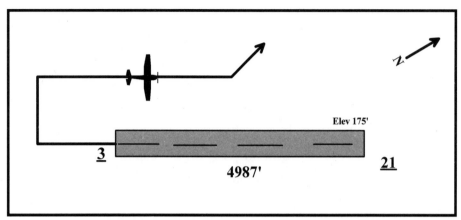

Figure 3.2.   Right Downwind departure.

12) Reduce power to about **"2300"** RPM at **"1000"** feet above the
    ground (AGL)
13) When you reach the midpoint of the runway, make a **LEFT**
    45 degree turn and depart the pattern

14) When wings are level, press **"P"** to pause the simulation

** 15) Record your:

ALTITUDE_____(20 pts)
AIRSPEED_____(20 pts)
VSI   _____(20 pts)
HEADING_____(15 pts)
FLAPS_____(10 pts)

16) Press **"P"** to continue the simulation

*"We're not in any rush to blast our way to altitude, so let's lower the
nose some, and increase our speed to 100 knots for the remainder of
the climb. By the way, that departure you did was the best one I've ever
seen you execute! Good job!"*

Climb out:

1) Increase your **AIRSPEED** to **"100"** knots

2) Continue your climb to "**3500**" feet and turn **RIGHT** to a heading of "**030**" (standard rate)

"Now, we're simply going to navigate on this 030 heading until intercepting the Van Nuys 140 radial. So keep your eye on that number one VOR!"

Level off:

1) Begin to level off when the altimeter reads "**3400**" feet
2) Maintain "**3500**" feet
3) Reduce power to about "**2200**" [**2400**] RPM
4) When the **NAV 1 CDI** is two dots **LEFT** of center, start your **RIGHT** turn to a heading of "**140**"
5) Start to roll out when you see "**130**" in the DG window
6) Track outbound on the **VAN NUYS VOR 140** radial

*"You are now set up to enter the LA TCA corridor. This corridor enables you to fly from the north side of Los Angeles, to the south side, without climbing to 12,500 feet. Good thing, huh?!! You must contact Los Angeles Approach Control on **134.9**, as it says on your Hollywood Park Route, to obtain permission to enter the corridor. And we'll go no farther than the Los Angeles 010 radial without a clearance. That is, if your NAV 2 CDI needle comes close to centering, make a 180 degree turn until you are cleared through the corridor. So let's do it now!"*

CORRIDOR -

1) Tune **COM** to "**134.9**" (LA Approach Control)

You:

"LOS ANGELES APPROACH, THIS IS CESSNA 13MIKE, WITH YOU AT 3500 FEET."

Los Angeles Approach:

"CESSNA 13MIKE, GO AHEAD."

You:

> **"13MIKE IS OVER CENTURY CITY, AND WOULD LIKE TO REQUEST A CLEARANCE FOR THE HOLLYWOOD PARK ROUTE TO TORRANCE AIRPORT."**

Los Angeles Approach:

> **"13MIKE, SQUAWK 3732 AND IDENT."**

> 2) Set **XPDR** to **"3732"** (assigned code) and you would push once the red IDENT button if you had one

You:

> **"13MIKE IS SQUAWKING 3732 AND IDENTING."**

Los Angeles Approach:

> **"13MIKE, RADAR CONTACT. YOU ARE CLEARED FROM PRESENT POSITION THROUGH THE LA VFR CORRIDOR TO TORRANCE AIRPORT. FLY HEADING OF 140 AND MAINTAIN 3500 FEET."**

You:

> **"13MIKE, CLEARED THROUGH THE CORRIDOR, 3500 FEET."**

"That was marvelous! Your radio communications were clear, concise, and Approach is probably having a party right now in celebration over your smoothness! Now, stay tight in your tracking outbound on the Van Nuys 140 radial because that's the corridor route. If you stray, believe me, Approach will let you know! But let's see if we can do this without their help!

> 3) Press **"P"** to pause the simulation

**   4) Record your:

NAV 1 DME DIST_____(25 pts)
NAV 2 DME DIST_____(25 pts)
ALTITUDE_____(20 pts)
AIRSPEED_____(15 pts)
XPDR _____(15 pts)
HEADING_____(15 pts)
VSI   _____(15 pts)

5) Press "**P**" to continue the simulation

6) Set **NAV 2 OBS** to "**076**" in the upper window

"Do you remember why we're doing this? We talked about it in our pre-brief in the Santa Monica lunchroom! This 076 radial from Los Angeles is a good point, while we're on the radial from Van Nuys, to break clear of the corridor route and come in on a nice 45 degree entry into Torrance for a right hand traffic pattern. It's easy to get behind with all this flurry of activity, but stay with it. You're the best!"

"We need to keep our eyes open and sharply peeled. The corridor is well traveled, so we need to exercise collision avoidance procedures."

Los Angeles Approach:

"CESSNA 13MIKE, SLOWER TRAFFIC AT YOUR TWO O'CLOCK POSITION."

You:

"13MIKE LOOKING."

"Okay, Do you see it? There he is, low at your two thirty position. It looks like a tail dragger. Got it? Good!"

You:

"LA APPROACH, 13MIKE HAS TRAFFIC."

7) Watch your **NAV 2 CDI**, when the needle is three dots right of center, call LA Approach

You:

"LOS ANGELES APPROACH, CESSNA 13MIKE AT 3500 FEET."

Los Angeles Approach:

"CESSNA 13MIKE, DO YOU HAVE TORRANCE AIRPORT IN SIGHT?"

You:

"13MIKE, THAT'S AFFIRMATIVE. REQUEST TO PROCEED DIRECT TO TORRANCE AT THIS TIME."

Los Angeles Approach:

"13MIKE, YOU'RE CLEARED DIRECT TO TORRANCE. SQUAWK 1200 AND GOOD DAY."

You:

"13MIKE, CLEARED DIRECT TORRANCE."

"All right, I'll tell you what! There's the airfield at our 2 o'clock position or so. Let's turn right to a heading of 195 degrees, and this should set us up nicely to turn onto the right 45 degree entry we've been talking about!"

8) When your **DG** reads "185" start to roll out
9) Maintain a heading of "195"
10) Reset **XPDR** to "1200" (VFR code)
11) Select "NAV 2" DME

Descent:

"We need to get a hold of Tower, but first you need to get what kind of information? That's right - ATIS! Frequency is 125.6."

    1) Tune **COM** to "**125.6**" (Torrance ATIS)

TORRANCE AIRPORT, INFORMATION LIMA, 1930 ZULU WEATHER, SKY CLEAR, VISIBILITY SIX, HAZE, TEMPERATURE 85, WIND 310 AT 7. ALTIMETER 29.94. LANDING AND DEPARTING RUNWAY 29 RIGHT. ADVISE ON INITIAL CONTACT YOU HAVE INFORMATION LIMA.

    2) Tune **COM** to "**124.0**" (Torrance Tower)

"Boy, are you sharp! You didn't even give me time to tell you to switch to Tower frequency that time! See how much more improved you're getting as we've progressed through this day? Let's see, you've got 124.0 - correct! While you're at it, go ahead and descend down to 1500 feet. Wait on calling Tower just yet."

    3) Set **ALTIMETER**, set **DG**, and check **FUEL**
    4) Set **CARB HEA**T to "**ON**"
    5) Reduce power to about "**1700**" **[2000]** RPM
    6) Descend to "**1500**" feet

"We're about seven miles from the airport - go ahead and call up Tower on 124.0. Professor Miller told you this would be short, didn't he?"

You:

    "TORRANCE TOWER, THIS IS CESSNA 13MIKE, OVER THE MOBIL REFINERY, DESCENDING TO 1500 FEET FOR LANDING, WITH INFORMATION LIMA."

Torrance Tower:

"CESSNA 13MIKE, YOU ARE CLEARED TO ENTER THE ATA, REPORT WHEN ON A THREE MILE RIGHT 45 FOR LANDING ON RUNWAY 29 RIGHT."

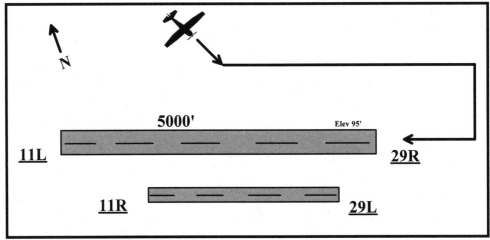

Figure 3.3. On 45 for Right Downwind runway 29R

You:

"13MIKE, WILL REPORT THREE MILE 45."

7) Press "**P**" to pause the simulation

** 8) Record your:

NAV 1 DME DIST_____(25 pts)
NAV 2 DME DIST_____(25 pts)
ALTITUDE_____(25 pts)
AIRSPEED_____(20 pts)
VSI   _____(20 pts)
HEADING_____(20 pts)

9) Press "**P**" to continue the simulation

Approach:

1) Approach the runway at a 45 degree angle (aim at the middle of the runway)
** 2) What would be the 45 degree heading to the midfield?
_____ (20 pts)

"Now it just so happens that three miles from the field is approximately 6.0 DME on your NAV 2, that is set for LAX VOR.. When you see 6.0, tell Tower your position."

You:

"TORRANCE TOWER, 13MIKE IS AT A THREE MILE RIGHT 45 FOR LANDING."

Torrance Tower:

"13MIKE, VISUAL CONTACT. PATTERN IS EMPTY. YOU ARE CLEARED FOR LANDING ON RUNWAY 29 RIGHT."

3) When your **NAV 2 DME DIST** reads "**7.0**" descend to "**1200**" feet
4) When your **NAV 2 DME DIST** reads "**7.3**" make a left turn to enter the **DOWNWIND** leg of the approach

"Ah! What a pretty sight to behold! Another airport - another landing - another beautiful view from the right side! This is the life, ain't it?!!!"

5) Reduce power to about "**1400**" **[1700]** RPM (this is the beginning of your approach descent)
6) Select **GEAR "DOWN"**
7) When you have slowed to **90 knots,** set **FLAPS** to **first notch** (10 degrees)
8) Try and maintain a **400** ft per minute descent on your Vertical Speed Indicator (VSI)

"I'm going to be quiet throughout most of this landing, just to see how you are in judging things for yourself. Just remember the basics of correcting while landing. Adjust height with power, and airspeed with pitch."

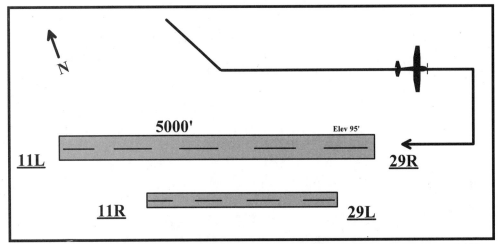

Figure 3.4.   Right Downwind turning Right Base runway 29R

9) When the end of the runway is at your 5 o'clock position, turn **RIGHT "90"** degrees to establish your **BASE** leg of the approach

10) Set **FLAPS** to **second notch** (20 degrees)

11) Press **"P"** to pause the simulation

**   12) Record your:

AIRSPEED_____	(25 pts)
VSI _____	(25 pts)
ALTITUDE_____	(25 pts)
RPM _____	(20 pts)
HEADING_____	(20 pts)
CARB HEAT_____	(15 pts)

13) Press **"P"** to continue the simulation

14) When runway 29R is at your 2 o'clock position, start a "**90**" degree **RIGHT** turn to establish your **FINAL** leg of the approach

"Sorry! But I've got to say it! You're doing good, but make sure that you make slight heading adjustments to compensate for winds, overshoots, or undershoots. You're still a teeny-weeny bit heavy handed on the yoke!"

15) When established on the **FINAL** leg, set **FLAPS** to **third notch** (30 degrees)
16) Airspeed should be **70 knots**
17) When the **ALTIMETER** displays "**400**" feet, press "**P**" to pause the simulation

**   18) Record your:

AIRSPEED_____(25 pts)
VSI   _____(25 pts)
HEADING_____(20 pts)
RPM   _____(15 pts)
FLAPS_____(15 pts)

19) Press "**P**" to continue simulation

20) When you are 10 to 20 feet off the runway, reduce power to about "**1000**" RPM and start to slowly pitch the nose of the aircraft up to slow your descent and establish a touchdown attitude

*"It's a good thing you love me despite my idiosyncrasies! But WATCH YOUR **AIRSPEED**! Be careful not to stall the aircraft. Make **60 knots** the airspeed of doom - no lower than that or else your sky hook snaps!"*

21) When you are five feet off the runway, hold the nose of the aircraft up and allow the airspeed to **SLOWLY** bleed off. Your aircraft will <u>settle</u> onto the runway while you follow the centerline

"Think of the Nutcracker Suite - it's a ballet move. Power - nose - let the airplane __settle__ onto the runway slowly. Keep your eyes looking down the runway slightly ahead."

22) After touchdown reduce power to **600 RPM**
23) Apply the brakes
24) Taxi the aircraft off the active runway to the left
25) When the aircraft has stopped, set **CARB HEAT** to "**OFF**"
26) Set **FLAPS** to "**0**"

"How do you feel? Isn't it exhilarating to know that you've done a fantastic job and put your whole mind and flying skills to the test? Take a break - I'll talk to Ground and taxi us in. You deserve the rest.

27) Tune **COM** to "**125.0**" (Torrance Ground)

Me:

"TORRANCE GROUND, CESSNA 13MIKE IS DOWN AND CLEAR OF RUNWAY 29 RIGHT FOR TAXI TO THE TERMINAL. I'D LIKE TO CLOSE MY VFR FLIGHT PLAN AT THIS TIME."

Torrance Ground:

"13MIKE, FLIGHT PLAN IS CLOSED, TAXI TO THE TERMINAL."

**   28) Record the **TIME**_____(5 pts)

TOTAL POINTS POSSIBLE FOR THIS SCENARIO __665__

✈ Flight Scenario Four

Torrance to Avalon

(Los Angeles Area - estimated flying time 30 minutes)

I don't hear the phone ringing, so I guess you didn't bust the TCA and no one has called me, Professor Miller, to complain about "13MIKE" wandering all over the sky. The last flight of the series takes you to wonderful Catalina Island, the land of romance and Buffalo Burgers. The approach to this airport is tricky, so stay alert, and do not be late on your power reductions or you may find yourself in trouble. If you just landed at Torrance, and you have talked Professor Calfior into joining you for a Buffalo Burger at the restaurant in Avalon, then you may skip the "SETUP" section and proceed to the "PREFLIGHT". If this is your first flight with "13MIKE" let me tell you how we do the setup. I will lead you through the initial setup phase of the flight simulator where you will set the aircraft type, winds, and position. I will show you how to save this setup so you may return to the Santa Monica Airport without going through the initial setup steps. I will then turn you over to Professor Calfior who will take you through the PREFLIGHT of "13MIKE" to set your instruments, TAXI, and perform a RUN UP of the engine prior to takeoff. He will instruct you in the TAKEOFF, CLIMB OUT, LEVEL OFF, COURSE CHANGES, DESCENT, APPROACH, and LANDING procedures that make up the bulk of this scenario. Please listen to what Professor Calfior has to say about flying techniques. He is trying to help you obtain the best possible score.

FLIGHT PLAN -

This flight begins with a departure from runway 29L at Torrance Airport, with a straight out departure climbing to 3500 feet. You will intercept the LOS ANGELES VOR 170 radial, and turn left to track outbound. After intercepting the SANTA CATALINA VOR 330 radial, you will perform a left turn to track inbound on that radial. Upon reaching five DME from the VOR, you will turn towards the airport and overfly the runway to enter a left downwind for runway 22. You will fly a standard left hand traffic pattern for landing at Avalon Airport. The aircraft will be low on fuel if you have flown the entire series of flights, so take your plane over to the refueling station and fill it up. After filling out our flight plan in Appendix A, and calling the Flight Service Station (FSS) to file it, we need to turn to Appendix B, and locate the sectional map for Los Angeles. Find Torrance and Avalon (on Catalina Island) airports. Draw the above route on the map. Now answer these questions.

**   a) Where can I get a good Buffalo Burger?

_____(15 pts)

**   b) Is the airport North or South of the town of Avalon?

_____(15 pts)

**   c) What is the altitude of the floor of the TCA at Torrance?

_____(15 pts)

SETUP

Aircraft:
　　1) Choose **"Cessna Skylane RG"**

Weather:
　　1) Set Surface winds **"DEPTH"** to **"1000"**
　　2) Set Surface winds **"DIR"** to **"270"**

3) Set Surface winds "**SPEED**" to "**10**"
4) Set Level 1 "**TOPS**" to "**10000**"
5) Set Level 1 "**BASE**" to "**1000**"
6) Set Level 1 "**DIR**" to "250"
7) Set Level 1 "**SPEED**" to "**15**"

Aircraft Position:

1) "**NORTH**" to "**15308.7247**" -- **[N033° 48' 12.8268]**
2) "**EAST**" to "**5815.3215**" -- **[W118° 20' 22.3438]**
3) "**ALTITUDE**" to "**108**" -- **[0]**
4) "**HEADING**" to "**200**"

note: At this point you may wish to save this setup for future use.

PREFLIGHT

note: Set **ZOOM** to "1.0"
Set **Time** to "13:00"

"I should be the one treating you to Buffalo Burgers, but since you offered first, I accept! Well, sad to say, but this is the final flight we'll spend together today in the Los Angeles area. Can you swim in case we run out of fuel over the water? Only kidding, we've got plenty! Well, I'm getting hungry, so let's get the ATIS information on 125.6. My guess is we'll takeoff on runway 29L or my name isn't Professor Calfior!"

Instruments:

1) Tune **COM** to "**125.6**" (ATIS)

"TORRANCE AIRPORT, INFORMATION DELTA, 2000 ZULU WEATHER, SKY CLEAR, VISIBILITY SEVEN IN HAZE. TEMPERATURE 85, WIND 270 AT 10. ALTIMETER 29.94. RUNWAY 29 LEFT IS ACTIVE FOR ALL DEPARTURES TO THE SOUTH, OTHERWISE DEPARTURES AND LANDINGS ARE ON RUNWAY 29 RIGHT.   ADVISE ON INITIAL CONTACT YOU HAVE INFORMATION DELTA."

"Now runway 29 left is pretty short - I guess that's relative if you're used to longer runways. Anyway, it's 3000 feet which is no problem for us. But I want you to always remember that computing takeoff distances is vital for each and every flight you accomplish.   Never take it for granted that you'll make it. Besides, FARs require you to compute all takeoff distances. Well, let's set up the instruments before taxiing."

    2) Set "**Altimeter**" and "**DG**"
    3) Set **XPDR** to "**1200**" (VFR code)
    4) Tune **NAV 1** to "**113.6**" (LAX)
    5) Set **NAV 1 OBS** to "**170**" in the upper window
    6) Tune **NAV 2** to "**111.4**" (SXC)
    7) Set **NAV 2 OBS** to "**150**" in the upper window
    8) Set the **DME** to "**NAV 1**" and "**DIST**"
    9) Check **CARB HEAT** is "**OFF**"
    10) Check **GEAR** "**DOWN**"
    11) Turn **STROBE** "**ON**"
    12) Check **LIGHTS** are "**OFF**"

*"Since we're just about ready to taxi, build another habit pattern. See that wind sock over there? Be figuring out which way the wind is blowing as you begin taxiing and make your turns, so that you can set up your ailerons and yoke accordingly. We certainly don't want a gust to flip us on our side simply because we forgot this procedure!" Ground is on, uh, **120.9** - am I right? Sure I'm right!"*

    13) Tune **COM** to "**120.9**" (Ground)

You:

    "TORRANCE GROUND, THIS IS CESSNA 13MIKE AT THE MID RAMP, READY TO TAXI WITH INFORMATION DELTA. SOUTHBOUND DEPARTURE."

Torrance Ground:

    "13MIKE, TAXI TO RUNWAY 29 LEFT AND ENJOY YOUR BURGERS!"

You:

    "13MIKE TAXIING."

TAXI -

    "You are facing the taxiway with runway 29R (right) at your back. Make a left 90 degree turn, and taxi down to the runup area just short of the takeoff end of runway 29L (left). Face the aircraft toward the runway but hold short of the runway. We'll do our runup checks here." See Figure 4.1.

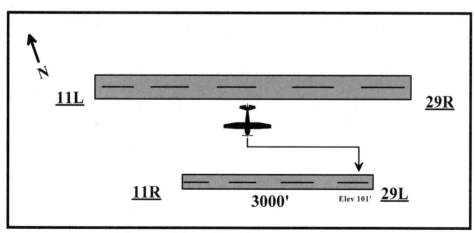

Figure 4.1.   Taxi to runway 29L

RUN UP -

    1) Set brake (hold down to prevent aircraft from moving)

    2) Advance power to about "**1700**" RPM

**   3) Select CARB HEAT "**ON**", record RPM drop_____(5 pts)

    4) Select CARB HEAT "**OFF**"

**   5) Select "**LEFT**" Mag, record RPM drop_____(5 pts)

    6) Select "**BOTH**" Mags

**   7) Select "**RIGHT**" Mag, record RPM drop_____(5 pts)

    8) Select "**BOTH**" Mags

    9) Reduce power to **idle**

    10) Set **FLAPS** to **first notch** (10 degrees takeoff configuration)

"This is just too exciting! No matter how many times I fly out to Catalina Island, it's a pure joy each and every time! This is your first time, so I'm sure you'll be absolutely flabbergasted when you see how beautiful this flight is! I'll tell you something unique about the runway we'll be landing on when we get closer to it! Keep you guessing and wondering - that's my job! Let's activate the flight plan with Ground."

You:

"TORRANCE GROUND, 13MIKE WOULD LIKE TO ACTIVATE ITS VFR FLIGHT PLAN TO AVALON AT THIS TIME."

Torrance Ground:

"13MIKE, YOUR FLIGHT PLAN IS ACTIVATED. SWITCH TO TOWER WHEN READY."

*"My mouth is starting to water already for that burger! Hurry up! Switch to **124.0** and get me to the restaurant!"*

    11) Tune **COM** to "**124.0**" (Torrance Tower)

You:

"TORRANCE TOWER, CESSNA 13MIKE, READY FOR SOUTHBOUND DEPARTURE RUNWAY 29 LEFT."

Torrance Tower:

> **"13MIKE, YOU ARE CLEARED FOR TAKEOFF. MAINTAIN RUNWAY HEADING UNTIL AT LEAST 1100 FEET, THEN FLY AS FILED."**

You:

> **"13MIKE CLEARED FOR TAKEOFF, STRAIGHT OUT DEPARTURE."**

FLIGHT

Takeoff:

"Good! A little scoot of power and keep us moving as we line up on the centerline of the runway. Remember - that's right - flaps are at 10 degrees, fuel is good, trimmed properly, oil temperature and pressure are within limits. Keep rolling and now go!"

1) Record TIME _____
2) Release brakes and taxi onto runway 29L
3) Advance power to **"FULL"**
4) Maintain centerline of runway
5) At **50 knots** airspeed lift nose wheel off runway
6) At **70 knots** ease back on the yoke to establish a 10 degree pitch up attitude
7) Maintain a climb **AIRSPEED** of **80 knots**
8) Raise **Gear** when there is no more runway to land on
9) At **"500"** feet above ground level raise the **FLAPS** to **"0"**
10) At **"1000"** feet AGL reduce power to about **"2300" RPM**

"Now that we're established in the climb, let's try an aileron roll! I'll bet you didn't know this puppy could do one, did you? Well, not very good - it stalls out when you're inverted, so maybe we better not try that just yet! Let's do like we did on the last flight, and lower our nose for a 100 knot climb to keep the engine cool."

Climb out:

1) Continue your climb to **"3500"** feet
2) Increase **AIRSPEED** to **"100"** knots

"It won't take long for you to intercept that 170 radial out of Los Angeles, so stay with this airplane. By the way, that takeoff was very well done!"

3) When the **NAV 1 CDI** is two and a half dots **RIGHT** of center, start a **LEFT** turn to a heading of **"170"**
4) Start to roll out when you see **"180"** in the **DG** window
5) Maintain a heading of **"170"** (watch the winds)
6) Track outbound on the **LOS ANGELES VOR 170** radial

** *"From the action of your Number 1 VOR CDI, from what direction is the wind blowing - LEFT or RIGHT?"*____(20 pts)

Level off:

1) Begin to level off when the altimeter reads **"3400"** feet
2) Maintain **"3500"** feet
3) Reduce power to about **"2200"** **[2400]** RPM
4) Press **"P"** to pause the simulation
** 5) Record your:

NAV 1 DME DIST_____(25 pts)
NAV 2 DME DIST_____(25 pts)
ALTITUDE_____(20 pts)
AIRSPEED_____(15 pts)
VSI   _____(15 pts)

6) Press **"P"** to continue the simulation

"Hey look! There's Flipper playing with Shamu!! Now, it's not like we have a wealth of visual landmarks here, but we have VORs! See how this all prepares you for instrument flying also, even though you're just flying visual? WOW, there's a mermaid!! Watch that Number 2 VOR - never mind the mermaid! Buffalo Burgers ho!!!"

Course change:

1) When the **NAV 2 CDI** needle is one half dot to the **RIGHT**, start a **LEFT** turn to a heading of "**150**"
2) Maintain "**3500**" feet and track inbound on the **SXC** "**330**" radial
3) Select **DME** "**NAV 2**"

"This time, do you have an airport traffic area to be concerned about? Ah, no you don't! Avalon has no control tower, so therefore it has no ATA. Got you! It does have a UNICOM, and I'd say about seven miles out from Santa Catalina VOR, let's call and give UNICOM our position and ask for the altimeter setting and active runway. It will be on frequency 122.7."

Descent:

1) When **NAV 2 DME DIST** reads "**7.0**", tune **COM** to "**122.7**" (Catalina UNICOM)

You:

"CATALINA UNICOM, CESSNA 13MIKE IS FIVE MILES NORTH AT 3500 FEET, FOR LANDING ADVISORY."

Catalina UNICOM:

"CESSNA 13MIKE, WINDS ARE 210 AT 8, RUNWAY 22 IS THE ACTIVE. TRAFFIC PATTERN ALTITUDE IS 2600 FEET, ALTIMETER IS 29.96. PATTERN IS EMPTY."

You:

"13MIKE WILL OVERFLY THE FIELD AT 2600 FEET, AND ENTER A LEFT DOWNWIND FOR RUNWAY 22."

2) Set **ALTIMETER**, set **DG**, and check **FUEL**
3) When **NAV 2 DME DIST** reads "**5.0**", set **CARB HEAT** to "**ON**" and reduce power to about "**1600**" [**1900**] RPM
4) Descend to "**2600**" feet

4

"That was well done. Since we're in the approach descent, let me tell you about the spared expenses of the runway. I'll tell you what! You tell me what you see as we overfly the field - that'll make it even more noteworthy for you!"

5) When **NAV 2 DME DIST** reads "**3.0**", turn left to "**140**" deg.

"Nice move there! I see you've adjusted your path so that you'll fly almost a right angle over the runway in order to have a nice 100 degree turn to the downwind. Good thinking! Go ahead and take some more power off - you don't need what you're carrying."

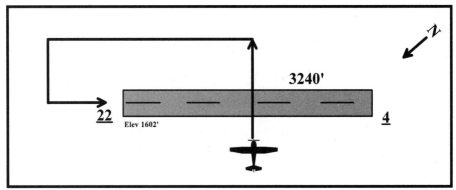

Figure 4.2. Overfly runway for Left Downwind runway 22

6) Reduce power to about "**1500**" **[1800]** RPM

*"HOLY COW!? Is that all you have to say about the runway - HOLY COW? It's got a few potholes and rough spots on it, doesn't it? Well, that's why I'd like you to do a soft field landing this time, so that we can cushion it somewhat. It's not too bad really, but just something for you to be aware of. Being on frequency **122.7**, who are we now concerned about talking to? That's right, any traffic that's out there - which we know ain't there, but give your reports anyway for those possibly arriving, who haven't called in yet."*

You:

> **"AVALON TRAFFIC, CESSNA 13MIKE IS OVERHEAD THE FIELD AND ENTERING A LEFT DOWNWIND FOR RUNWAY 22 - AVALON."**

Approach:

1) When you are over the runway, set **GEAR "DOWN"**
2) When you have slowed to **90 knots**, set **FLAPS** to **first notch**
3) After overflying the runway, give yourself room before turning downwind so you are not too close to the runway

"Stay at 2600 feet until you get abeam of your point of intended landing. Good - that's great! Watch your distance from the runway off your left side. It's looking a little bit wide, so bring it in just a scooch. What's a scooch, you say? Come on, it's the same thing as a phlegma! You young kids don't hardly know anything about good speaking nowadays!"

4) Press **"P"** to pause the simulation
** 5) Record your:

ALTITUDE_____	(25 pts)
VSI_____	(25 pts)
RPM_____	(20 pts)
AIRSPEED_____	(20 pts)
HEADING_____	(15 pts)
CARB HEAT_____	(10 pts)

6) Press **"P"** to continue simulation

You:

> **"AVALON TRAFFIC, CESSNA 13MIKE IS ON LEFT DOWNWIND FOR RUNWAY 22, FULL STOP, AVALON."**

7) When abeam the approach end, reduce power to about **"1400"** **[1700]** RPM and try to maintain a **400** ft per minute descent rate

4

8) When the end of the runway is at your 7 o'clock position, turn **LEFT "90"** degrees to establish your **BASE** leg of the approach

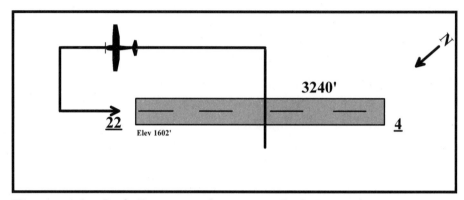

Figure 4.3. Left Downwind turning Left Base for runway 22

You:

"AVALON TRAFFIC, CESSNA 13MIKE IS ON LEFT BASE FOR RUNWAY 22, FULL STOP, AVALON."

9) Set **FLAPS** to **second notch** (20 degrees)
10) When runway 22 is at your 10 o'clock position, start a **"90"** degree **LEFT** turn to establish your **FINAL** leg of the approach

You:

"AVALON TRAFFIC, CESSNA 13MIKE IS ON FINAL FOR RUNWAY 22, FULL STOP, AVALON."

"You're just a tiny bit off that centerline. Make slight heading adjustments to compensate for the winds, which cause those inadvertent overshoots or undershoots."

11) When established on the **FINAL** leg, set **FLAPS** to **third notch** (30 degrees)
12) Airspeed should be **70 knots**

"This is the last time you'll hear me say this today! Adjust height with power, and airspeed with pitch. I'd simply feel incomplete if I didn't harp on that, and nag you about it!!!"

13) When the altimeter displays "**1900**" feet, press "**P**" to pause the simulation

** 14) Record your:

AIRSPEED_____(20 pts)

VSI_____(20 pts)

HEADING_____(15 pts)

RPM _____(15 pts)

FLAPS_____(15 pts)

15) Press "**P**" to continue the simulation

*"A soft field landing is exactly the same as a normal landing, except you will carry a little more power, like about **1200 RPM**, to cushion it. We should hardly even know that we've touched down. Also, hold that nose up as long as you can until it must fall down on your rollout."*

16) When you are 10 to 20 feet off the runway, reduce power to about "**1200**" RPM, and start to slowly pitch the nose of the aircraft up to slow your descent and establish a touchdown attitude.

*"WATCH YOUR **AIRSPEED**! The same restrictions apply as with a normal landing. Be careful not to stall the aircraft. Don't let your airspeed drop below **60 knots**. If it does, Shamu leaps out of the water, eats you up, and I don't get my free Buffalo Burger! So, a lot is riding on this for me!"*

17) When you are five feet off the runway, hold the nose of the aircraft up and allow the airspeed to **SLOWLY** bleed off. Your aircraft will <u>settle</u> onto the runway while you follow the centerline.

4

*"Easy, easy! Of course you'll float down the runway more than normal because of the bit of additional power you have. Don't be impatient, let the aircraft **settle** onto the runway slowly."*

18) After touchdown, reduce power to **600 RPM**
19) Apply the brakes
20) Taxi the aircraft off the active runway to the left
21) Stop on the taxiway and set **CARB HEAT** to **"OFF"**
22) Set **FLAPS** to **"0"**

"What a garden spot! Don't forget to transmit that you're off the active. We'll need some fuel. Hey, look at the UNICOM operator waving at us from his building! He better not say the restaurant is out of Buffalo Burgers!!"

You:

"AVALON TRAFFIC, CESSNA 13MIKE IS CLEAR OF THE ACTIVE, WILL TAXI FOR FUEL."

23) Taxi to the large square with an "F" in the middle of the square
24) Upon arrival at the fuel station, set brake, turn **STROBE** **"OFF"**, and turn **MAGS** to **"LEAN"** to shut down your engine

"We'll close our flight plan from a phone inside. I've got to call my wife anyway to tell her we didn't get eaten up by ORCA the killer whale! What say we go in and feed both, this old flight instructor, and pilot extraordinaire!!! I think I hear those woolly beasts calling us!!"

** 25) Record the **TIME**_____(5 pts)

TOTAL POSSIBLE POINTS FOR THIS FLIGHT IS __**385**__

✈ Flight Scenario Five

Lansing to Aurora

(Chicago Area - estimated flying time 30 minutes)

Professor Miller with you once again! If you have had enough flying in the smog of the Los Angeles area, let's try a little northern flying. Let me tell you about the first flight of Series Number Two. It departs Lansing Municipal in the southeast portion of Chicago and arrives at Aurora Municipal in the southwest portion of Chicago. If this is your first flight with "13MIKE", let me tell you how we do the setup. I will lead you through the initial setup phase of the flight simulator where you will set the aircraft type, winds, and position. I will show you how to save this setup so you may return to the Lansing Airport without going through the initial setup again. I will then turn you over to Professor Calfior who will take you through the PREFLIGHT of "13MIKE" to set your instruments, TAXI, and perform a RUN UP of the engine prior to takeoff. He will instruct you in the TAKEOFF, CLIMB OUT, LEVEL OFF, COURSE CHANGES, DESCENT, APPROACH, and LANDING procedures that make up the bulk of this scenario. Please listen to what Professor Calfior has to say about flying techniques. He is trying to help you obtain the best possible score.

FLIGHT PLAN -

The scenario begins with a departure from runway 36 at Lansing Municipal, with a climb out to 4500 feet. After departure, you will be turning to a heading of 260 and then proceed inbound on the JOLIET 086 radial. Upon crossing JOLIET, you will fly outbound on the JOLIET 330 radial and set up for a straight in landing on Aurora's runway 36. After filling out our flight plan in Appendix A, and calling the Flight Service Station (FSS) to file it, we need to turn to Appendix B, and locate the sectional map for Chicago. Find Lansing and Aurora airports. Draw the above route on the map. Now answer these questions.

** a) Just before you get to JOLIET VOR, what is the name of the airport
   to your left?_____(15 pts)

** b) What is the name of the VOR just to your left as you depart Lansing?
   _____ (15 pts)

** c) Do you need to fly under the Chicago TCA anywhere along your
   route of flight?_____ (15 pts)

SETUP

Aircraft:
   1) Choose **"Cessna Skylane RG"**

Weather:
   1) Set Surface winds **"DEPTH"** to **"1200"**
   2) Set Surface winds **"DIR"** to **"020"**
   3) Set Surface winds **"SPEED"** to **"7"**
   4) Set Level 1 **"TOPS"** to **"8000"**
   5) Set Level 1 **"BASE"** to **"1200"**
   6) Set Level 1 **"DIR"** to **"070"**
   7) Set Level 1 **"SPEED"** to **"20"**

Aircraft Position:
1) "**NORTH**" to "**17051.8834**" -- [N041° 32' 19.7426]
2) "**EAST**" to "**16696.8679**" -- [W087° 31' 48.9605]
3) "**ALTITUDE**" to "**619**" -- [0]
4) "**HEADING**" to "**270**"

note: At this point you may wish to save this setup for future use.

PREFLIGHT

note: Set **ZOOM** to "1.0"
Set **TIME** to "10:00"

*"Well, Professor Miller - I guess it's time for me to go to work! Thank you for giving my student your excellent presentation and briefing. I'm Professor Calfior. I'm anticipating a great, maybe even an outstanding flight with you. I'd certainly enjoy having you fly the entire circuit with me until we get back to Meigs Field in Chicago. Anyway, let's get the local airport information before we start to taxi, from the UNICOM operator here on the field. It's on **122.7**."*

Instruments:

1) Tune **COM** to "122.7" (Lansing UNICOM)

You:

"LANSING UNICOM, CESSNA 13MIKE IS ON THE RAMP AND WOULD LIKE SOME NUMBERS BEFORE TAXIING."

Lansing UNICOM:

"13MIKE, WHAT I'VE GOT IS GARY'S ALTIMETER SETTING OF 30.02. I SHOW WINDS FROM THE NORTHEAST AT 020, ABOUT SEVEN OR SO KNOTS. RUNWAY 36 IS THE RUNWAY IN USE FOR TAKEOFF IF YOU DON'T MIND TURF!"

You:

"THANKS A LOT, UNICOM! YOU'RE A BIG HELP, TURF WILL BE GOOD PRACTICE. ENJOY YOUR DAY!"

"Well, good! Let me watch you set up your instruments in accordance to what we pre-briefed the flight to be, and then we'll taxi out to 36."

2) Set "**Altimeter**"
3) Set "**DG**"
4) Set **XPDR** to "**1200**" (VFR code)
5) Tune **NAV 1** to "**112.3**" (JOT)
6) Set **NAV 1 OBS** to "**266**" in the upper window
7) Tune **NAV 2** to "**112.3**" (JOT)
8) Set **NAV 2 OBS** to "**330**" in the upper window
9) Set the **DME** to "**NAV 1**" and "**DIST**"
10) Check **CARB HEAT** is "**OFF**"
11) Check **GEAR** "**DOWN**"
12) Turn **STROBE** "**ON**"
13) Check **LIGHTS** "**OFF**"

"Excellent! The advantage of having two VORs, obviously, is so that we don't have to juggle so much going from one radial to another! Stay on this frequency and simply let traffic know that we're taxiing to runway 36. It's a good communication habit to get into."

You:

"LANSING TRAFFIC, CESSNA 13MIKE IS TAXIING TO RUNWAY 36."

TAXI -

"Runway 36 is behind you. Make a left turn and taxi down to the runup area for runway 36. Hold short of the runway and perform your runup. See Figure 5.1."

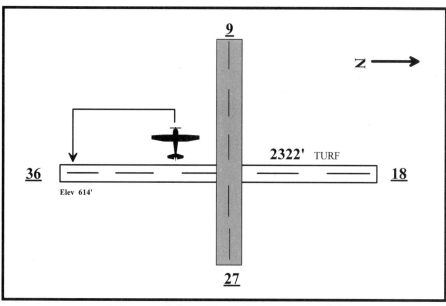

Figure 5.1.   Taxi to runway 36

RUN UP -

          1) Set brake (hold down to prevent aircraft from moving)

          2) Advance power to about **"1700"** RPM

**   3) Select CARB HEAT **"ON"**, record RPM drop_____(5 pts)

          4) Select CARB HEAT **"OFF"**

**   5) Select **"LEFT"** Mag, record RPM drop_____(5 pts)

          6) Select **"BOTH"** Mags

**   7) Select **"RIGHT"** Mag, record RPM drop_____(5 pts)

          8) Select **"BOTH"** Mags

          9) Reduce power to **idle**

          10) Set **FLAPS** to **first notch** (10 degrees takeoff configuration)

"All right! You've already called Kankakee's Flight Service Station on the phone to activate our flight plan, so all that's left to do is to clear this approach end, and make sure nobody's coming in. Let traffic know we're taking the active for takeoff."

You:

"LANSING TRAFFIC, CESSNA 13MIKE IS ROLLING ON RUNWAY 36 FOR TAKEOFF. WESTBOUND DEPARTURE."

FLIGHT

Takeoff:

"Flap settings are checked at 10 degrees, we're full on fuel - check it, trimmed for takeoff, oil temperature and pressure are in limits - yeah, as long as you see the needles on the green, you're okay. Verify no traffic on final once more - go for it!"

1) Record TIME _____
2) Release brakes and taxi onto runway 36
3) Advance power to **"FULL"**
4) Maintain centerline of runway
5) At **50 knots** airspeed lift nose wheel off runway
6) At **70 knots** ease back on the yoke to establish a 10 degree pitch up attitude
7) Maintain a climb **AIRSPEED** of **80 knots**
8) Raise **Gear** when there is no more runway to land on
9) At **"500"** feet above the ground raise the **FLAPS** to **"0"**
10) Reduce power to about **"2300"** RPM at **"1000"** feet above the ground (AGL)

*"This should give you approximately an **"800"** feet per minute climb rate on your Vertical Speed Indicator (VSI). You're looking solid here!"*

Climb out:

1) Maintain runway heading and climb to **"2000"** feet
2) At **"2000"** feet, start a climbing **LEFT** turn to a heading of **"266"**

"All your turns should be STANDARD RATE. You make a STANDARD RATE turn by keeping the wings on the little airplane displayed on the TURN COORDINATOR aligned with the "L" indicator. It's easy to overbank, but keep that control in your scan as well as looking out for other traffic. That's it! Keep your head on a swivel!!"

    3) Start to roll out when you see "**275**" in the **DG** window
    4) Maintain a heading of "**266**"

"Yeah boy! You just keep that heading steady, unless you notice that the winds at altitude here are pulling you off the ground track you've planned for. Check your landmarks."

    5) Track inbound on the "**086**" radial (266 course) that your
       NAV 1 OBI is displaying

"To track inbound on a VOR radial, you keep the CDI needle centered by making minor heading changes to compensate for winds. If the needle goes off to the left side, it's a left correction, if it goes right, it's a right correction."

Level off:

    1) Begin to level off when the altimeter reads "**4400**" feet
    2) Maintain "**4500**" feet
    3) Reduce power to about "**2200**" **[2400]** RPM

Course change:

"You should be fairly stabilized by now with that centered needle, so let's see what we've got. According to the winds aloft forecast, we had winds at altitude of about 070 at 20 knots, right? Don't we expect a bit of a right correction and an impressive ground speed?"

**   1) At "**20**" **DME**, record your ground speed _____, (25 pts)
       and heading _____, (25 pts) for a centered CDI needle

**   2) How many other airports can you see easily somewhere along your en route track to JOLIET VOR? _____on the left (15 pts) - _____on the right (15 pts)

"As we get closer and closer to Joliet VOR, be thinking ahead to your course change and when you want to initiate it. You're only turning approximately 60 degrees, so not much lead is necessary - maybe when your Number 1 DME reads 0.7 or 0.8. Keep looking outside for traffic! We don't want any surprise visits in our cockpit!!!!"

     3) Watch your **DIST** on the **NAV 1 DME,** and when it reads "**0.7**" then commence your **RIGHT** turn to a heading of "**330**"

     4) When your heading indicator reads "**320**", start to roll out

     5) After you have rolled out, press "**P**" to pause the simulation

**   6) Record your:

         NAV 1 DME DIST_____(25 pts)
         ALTITUDE_____(20 pts)
         AIRSPEED_____(15 pts)
         VSI_____(15 pts)
         GEAR_____(10 pts)
         FLAPS_____(10 pts)
         MAGS_____(10 pts)
         STROBE_____(10 pts)
         LIGHTS_____(10 pts)

     7) Press "**P**" to continue the simulation

     8) Track outbound on the "**330**" radial that your **NAV 2 OBI** is displaying

"Just to get a little more specific with you on these corrections, if you constantly drift to the left, as it seems is happening, then you need to make a wind correction to your current planned heading. Try and offset to the right about 20 degrees in order to get that needle moving back towards the center. Once centered, take half that correction out and see what happens."

Descent:

1) When established outbound, reduce power to about "**1900**" [**2100**] RPM, descend and maintain "**2300**" feet

*"Whenever we descend, it's not like we want to imitate a rock! A nice average control rate of descent is about **700** feet per minute in the en route structure, so let's shoot for that."*

2) Tune **NAV 1** to "**108.4**" (DPA) and set the **DME** to "**NAV 2**"

3) Set **NAV 1 OBS** to "**002**" in the upper window

4) Watch your **NAV 1 CDI**, and when the needle is centered, press "**P**" to pause the simulation

** 5) Record your:

NAV 2 DME_____(25 pts)
NAV 1 DME _____(25 pts)
HEADING_____(20 pts)
ALTITUDE_____(20 pts)
VSI_____(15 pts)
AIRSPEED_____(15 pts)

6) Press "**P**" to continue the simulation

*"Do you see what we're doing? We're simply heading north and orienting ourselves for the expected approach into Aurora's runway 36, since winds are probably close to the same as they were in Lansing. In a little while, I want you to get the airport information from Lansing's Automatic Terminal Information Service which is called **ATIS**. As a matter of fact, let's do that now on **125.85**, so that we can call Aurora Tower and not rush."*

7) Tune **COM** on "**125.85**" (Aurora ATIS)

5

"AURORA MUNICIPAL, INFORMATION INDIA, 1500 WEATHER, SKY CLEAR, VISIBILITY 35. TEMPERATURE 81, WIND 010 AT 8. ALTIMETER 30.00. LANDING AND DEPARTING RUNWAY 36. ADVISE ON INITIAL CONTACT YOU HAVE INFORMATION INDIA."

"Just as I thought! Okay, just as we thought! Let's fly to our next checkpoint."

    8) Set **NAV 1 OBS** to "**014**" and commence a further descent to "**2000**" feet

    9) Set **ALTIMETER**, set **DG**, and check **FUEL**

*"Before we cruise into the airport traffic area's five mile radius, since there's a tower, we need to call tower and get cleared in. According to your sectional, tower is on **120.6**, and keep your eye on that Number 1 needle. Let tower know where you are and altitude."*

    10) Tune **COM** to "**120.6**" (Aurora Tower)

You:

"AURORA TOWER, THIS IS CESSNA 13MIKE, ABOUT SEVEN MILES SOUTH OF THE FIELD, DESCENDING TO 2000 FEET, INBOUND FOR LANDING WITH INDIA. REQUEST A STRAIGHT IN TO A FULL STOP, RUNWAY 36."

Aurora Tower:

"CESSNA 13MIKE, CONTINUE INBOUND AND REPORT WHEN FOUR MILES FROM THE FIELD. A STRAIGHT IN IS APPROVED, BUT BE ADVISED OF POSSIBILITY OF THE NEED TO ADJUST SPEED DUE TO NUMEROUS AIRCRAFT IN THE PATTERN."

You:

"13MIKE, WILL REPORT FOUR MILES."

11) Watch your **NAV 1 CDI**, when the needle again centers, press "**P**" to pause the simulation

** 12) Record your:

NAV 2 DME_____(25 pts)
NAV 1 DME_____(25 pts)
ALTITUDE_____(20 pts)
AIRSPEED_____(20 pts)
IS THE FIELD IN SIGHT?_____(15 pts)

13) Press "**P**" to continue the simulation

Approach:

"You will now start your long "FINAL" leg of the approach, also known as a straight in approach. You should be able to see Aurora Municipal's runway 36. That centered needle corresponds real close to being about four miles from the field, so hail them with the good news!"

You:

"AURORA TOWER, 13MIKE IS ON A FOUR MILE FINAL FOR A FULL STOP ON RUNWAY 36."

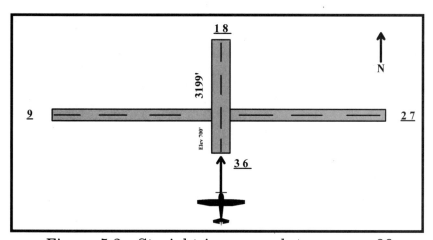

Figure 5.2. Straight in approach to runway 36

Aurora Tower:

> **"13MIKE, HAVE YOU IN SIGHT. YOUR TRAFFIC IS ON A ONE MILE FINAL FOR A TOUCH AND GO, FOLLOW HIM. YOU ARE CLEARED FOR A FULL STOP LANDING."**

You:

> **"13MIKE, CLEARED TO LAND. TRAFFIC IN SIGHT."**

> 1) **CARB HEAT "ON"**
> 2) Select **GEAR "DOWN"**
> 3) Reduce power to about **"1400" [1700]** RPM

"We're coming in slightly from the right, aren't we? So correct to the left to line up on runway 36, and keep that touchdown area of the runway fixed on the lower segment of your windscreen as a visual reference. We need to slow to 90 knots, so we can get some flaps in. Very smooth flying - you're quite enjoyable to fly with!"

> 4) When you have slowed to **90 knots,** set **FLAPS** to **first notch** (10 degrees)
> 5) Try and maintain a **400** ft per minute descent on your Vertical Speed Indicator (VSI)
> 6) When the **NAV 1 DME** reads **"11.3",** set **FLAPS** to **second notch** (20 degrees)

"This is looking wunderbar! Prima! Rad! Cool! Hep! Well, watch your descent - all you need is about 400 feet per minute. Remember, control is the key. Try and maintain the same runway aspect as you continue your descent. Don't let the runway rise or fall."

> 7) When the altimeter displays **"1100"** feet, set **FLAPS** to **third notch** (30 degrees), airspeed should be **70** knots

"Oh, I can say these following words in my sleep! But I want you to think of these words as naturally as breathing when you're in the landing phase. Adjust height with power, and airspeed with pitch. Hold the yoke lightly so you don't gorilla paw the corrections!

8) Press "**P**" to pause the simulation

**   9) Record your:

AIRSPEED_____(25 pts)
VSI_____(25 pts)
HEADING_____(20 pts)
RPM_____(20 pts)
FLAPS_____(15 pts)
GEAR_____(15 pts)

10) Press "**P**" to continue the simulation

11) When you are 10 to 20 feet off the runway, reduce power to about "**1000**" RPM, and start to slowly pitch the nose of the aircraft up to slow your descent and establish a touchdown attitude

*"10 to 20 feet is still a long way to fall, so WATCH YOUR **AIRSPEED**! Be careful not to stall the aircraft. Don't let your airspeed drop below **60 knots**. As long as you're holding your landing attitude prior to this, and the runway is still fixed on your windscreen, only getting bigger, you'll always be safe with your speed."*

12) When you are five feet off the runway, hold the nose of the aircraft up and allow the airspeed to **SLOWLY** bleed off. Your aircraft will settle onto the runway while you follow the centerline.

"That's it! Do this with the speed of smoothness. Treat it with a velvet touch. Don't be impatient! Just let the aircraft settle onto the runway slowly."

5

13) After touchdown, reduce power to **600 RPM**
14) Apply the brakes
15) Turn left and taxi off the active runway
16) When aircraft has stopped, set **CARB HEAT** to "OFF"
17) Set **FLAPS** to "0"

*"Did I ever enjoy that landing! I'm telling you, that was a masterpiece! We've still got some things to do and take care of. One of which is to switch to Ground Control on **121.7** and get our taxi clearance to the terminal. I'm parched for a Wal-Mart Sam's Choice Free & Clear Strawberry Low-Calorie Sparkling Flavored Beverage! No, a Wal-Mart isn't here, but I brought a bottle with me! Let's close your flight plan after you get inside, you can use the phone."*

18) Tune **COM** to "121.7" (Aurora Ground)

You:

"AURORA GROUND, CESSNA 13MIKE IS DOWN AND CLEAR OF RUNWAY 36 FOR TAXI TO THE TERMINAL."

Aurora Ground:

"13MIKE, TAXI TO THE TERMINAL."

**   19) Record the **TIME** _____(5 pts)

TOTAL POINTS POSSIBLE FOR THIS FLIGHT__ **615** __

Flight Scenario Six

Aurora to Bloomington-Normal

(Chicago Area - estimated flying time 45 minutes)

Calling all aircraft! Calling all aircraft! Has anybody seen Professor Miller? Oh, that's me! Yikes! It sure is windy around these parts. I guess you found that out on the last flight. I hope you keep that in mind when you fly this next scenario. This is the second flight of the Chicago area series. This flight can be flown as a continuation of the first flight, which began at Lansing Municipal, in the southeast portion of the Chicago area and arrived at Aurora Municipal in the southwest portion of Chicago. It may also be flown as a complete self contained flight. If you and Professor Calfior are continuing on to Bloomington-Normal, then you may skip the "SETUP" section and proceed to the "PREFLIGHT". If this is your first flight with "13MIKE", let me tell you how we do the setup. I will lead you through the initial setup phase of the flight simulator where you will set the aircraft type, winds, and position. I will show you how to save this setup so you may return to the Aurora Airport without going through the initial setup steps. I will then turn you over to Professor Calfior who will take you through the PREFLIGHT of "13MIKE" to set your instruments, TAXI, and perform a RUN UP of the engine prior to takeoff. He will instruct you in the TAKEOFF, CLIMB OUT, LEVEL OFF, COURSE CHANGES, DESCENT, APPROACH, and LANDING procedures that make up the bulk of this scenario. And do listen to what Professor Calfior has to say about flying techniques. He is trying to help you obtain the best possible score.

FLIGHT PLAN -

The route of flight follows well established departure, climb, cruise, descent, and landing procedures. The procedures begin with a departure from runway 36 at Aurora Municipal, with a climb out to 3000 feet. From midfield on the downwind leg, you will fly on a 225 magnetic heading until intercepting the JOLIET 290 radial. Then you will turn left to a heading of 210, continue climb to 4500 feet, and maintain that heading until intercepting the JOLIET 256 radial. Proceed inbound on the PONTIAC 348 radial, and descend down to 3500 feet. When over PONTIAC VOR, fly outbound on the PONTIAC 182 radial until you intercept the BLOOMINGTON 060 radial, where you turn right for a 45 degree entry to enter a left hand traffic pattern for landing on runway 11. After filling out our flight plan in Appendix A, and calling the Flight Service Station (FSS) to file it, we need to turn to Appendix B, and locate the sectional map for Chicago. Find Aurora and Blomington-Normal airports. Draw the above route on the map. Now answer these questions.

**   a) What is the name of the airport on the tracks, as you cross the 290
        radial of Joliet?_____(15 pts)
**   b) What's the name of the river you cross, as you head south to Pontiac
        VOR?   _____(15 pts)
**   c) What interstate do you parallel and cross, inbound from Pontiac VOR
        to your destination?_____(15 pts)

SETUP

Aircraft:
   1) Choose **"Cessna Skylane RG"**

Weather:
   1) Set Surface winds **"DEPTH"** to **"1200"**
   2) Set Surface winds **"DIR"** to **"020"**
   3) Set Surface winds **"SPEED"** to **"7"**

4) Set Level 1 "**TOPS**" to "**8000**"
5) Set Level 1 "**BASE**" to "**1200**"
6) Set Level 1 "**DIR**" to "**070**"
7) Set Level 1 "**SPEED**" to "**20**"

Aircraft Position:
1) "**NORTH**" to "**17151.8240**" -- [N041° 46' 17.4125]
2) "**EAST**" to "**16392.8698**" -- [W088° 28' 19.7892]
3) "**ALTITUDE**" to "**711**" -- [0]
4) "**HEADING**" to "**180**"

note: At this point you may wish to save this setup for future use.

PREFLIGHT

note: Set **ZOOM** to "**1.0**"
Set **TIME** to "**12:00**"

"Ah, lunch just hit the spot! So we're heading south, are we? I'm Professor Calfior. If you're writing me a check, call me Fred! I'm your friend indeed!!! To get out of here, we need to know some things from our neighboring ATIS recording on 125.85. Dial it into the communications panel, and listen to the informational melody of wisdom and knowledge from those in the know!"

6

Instruments:

1) Tune **COM** to "**125.85**" (ATIS)

"AURORA MUNICIPAL, INFORMATION JULIETTE, 1700 ZULU WEATHER, SKY CLEAR WITH A FEW ISOLATED AND SCATTERED SHOWERS TO THE NORTHWEST. TEMPERATURE 85, WIND 020 AT 10. ALTIMETER 29.98. LANDING AND DEPARTING RUNWAY 36 OR RUNWAY 9 FOR INSTRUMENT APPROACH PROCEDURES. STATE DESIRED DIRECTION OF DEPARTURE TO GROUND CONTROL. ADVISE ON INITIAL CONTACT YOU HAVE INFORMATION JULIETTE."

"Even though runway 9 is longer and better looking, we'll jump out of here from runway 36 for convenience sake. Shall we handle the instrument setup before we roll? Yeah, I think that's a good idea too, just because I said it! When you're an instructor, you can say that too, with pure egotistical satisfaction and questionable bravado!!!"

2) Set "**Altimeter**" and set "**DG**"
3) Set **XPDR** to "**1200**" (VFR code)
4) Tune **NAV 1** to "**112.3**" (JOT)
5) Set **NAV 1 OBS** to "**290**" in the upper window
6) Tune **NAV 2** to "**109.6**" (PNT)
7) Set **NAV 2 OBS** to "**168**" in the upper window
8) Set the **DME** to "**NAV 1**" and "**DIST**"
9) Check **CARB HEAT** is "**OFF**"
10) Check **GEAR** "**DOWN**"
11) Turn **STROBE** "**ON**"
12) Check **LIGHTS** are "**OFF**"

*"Now when you talk to Aurora Ground on **121.7**, make sure they know our intentions are to taxi to runway 36, and that we want a left downwind departure. Then we'll be flying exactly as we've got planned. If they assign us any other way, that's the life of a pilot - we'll figure it out!!!"*

13) Tune **COM** to "**121.7**" (Aurora Ground)

You:

> "AURORA GROUND, THIS IS CESSNA 13MIKE AT THE TERMINAL FOR TAXI TO RUNWAY 36 WITH A LEFT DOWNWIND DEPARTURE. I HAVE INFORMATION JULIETTE."

Aurora Ground:

> "13MIKE, TAXI TO RUNWAY 36. NEW ALTIMETER SETTING IS 29.97."

You:

> "13MIKE, 29.97."

TAXI -

> *"The runway is to your left. Taxi straight ahead until you reach the runup area which is just a hop, skip, and jump away if you're a rabbit! Turn the aircraft towards the runway, but not on it. We will do the runup from there."* See Figure 6.1

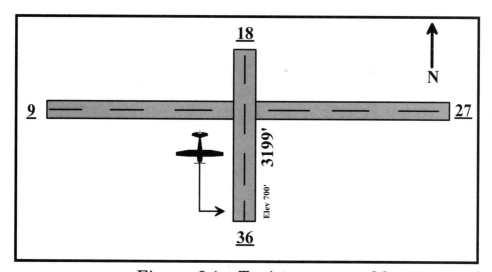

Figure 6.1. Taxi to runway 36.

RUN UP -

1) Set brake (hold down to prevent aircraft from moving)
2) Advance power to about **"1700"** RPM
** 3) Select CARB HEAT **"ON"**, record RPM drop_____(5 pts)
4) Select CARB HEAT **"OFF"**
** 5) Select **"LEFT"** Mag, record RPM drop_____(5 pts)
6) Select **"BOTH"** Mags
** 7) Select **"RIGHT"** Mag, record RPM drop_____(5 pts)
8) Select **"BOTH"** Mags
9) Reduce power to **idle**
10) Set **FLAPS** to **first notch** (10 degrees takeoff configuration)

"What do we need to activate? No, not the autopilot! Try again! No, not the Super Nintendo Martyr Brothers, or whoever they are! No, not the Romulan Cloaking Device! You got it! You filed it, since you went through the trouble of putting it together, you might as well use it! Let's activate the VFR flight plan right here with Ground."

You:

"AURORA GROUND, 13MIKE WOULD LIKE TO ACTIVATE ITS VFR FLIGHT PLAN TO BLOOMINGTON-NORMAL AS OF 1207 LOCAL."

Aurora Ground:

"13MIKE, YOUR VFR FLIGHT PLAN IS ACTIVATED. FLY SAFE AND HAVE A GOOD DAY."

You:

"13MIKE."

"Wait! I've got to put my '13MIKE' hat on before we move! If you can land at Bloomington without scaring me, I'll give you one of your own! Okay, now go to Tower on 120.6. I'm sure Ground has passed on our intentions to them. Let's test it out."

11) Tune **COM** to "**120.6**" (Aurora Tower)

You:

> "AURORA TOWER, CESSNA 13MIKE, READY FOR DEPARTURE RUNWAY 36."

Aurora Tower:

> "CESSNA 13MIKE, HOLD SHORT FOR TRAFFIC ON SHORT FINAL."

You:

> "13MIKE, HOLDING SHORT."

Aurora Tower:

> "13MIKE, YOU ARE NOW CLEARED FOR TAKEOFF, LEFT DOWNWIND DEPARTURE APPROVED. MAINTAIN RUNWAY HEADING TILL 1400 FEET."

You:

> "13MIKE IS CLEARED FOR TAKEOFF. ROLLING."

FLIGHT

6

Takeoff:

"Have you got a handle on this left downwind departure drill? Good! Add some power to get on the runway and at the same time, check your flaps to make sure they're in place at 10 degrees, fuel is okay, trim set, oil temperature and pressure are in the green - nothing seems to be stopping us. Let'er rip 13MIKE!"

1) Record TIME _____

2) Release brakes and taxi onto runway

3) Advance power to "**FULL**"

4) Maintain centerline of runway

5) At **50 knots** airspeed lift nose wheel off runway

6) At **70 knots** ease back on the yoke to establish a 10 degree pitch up attitude

7) Maintain a climb **AIRSPEED** of **80 knots**

8) Raise **Gear** when there is no more runway to land on

9) At "**500**" feet above the ground raise the **FLAPS** to "**0**"

** 10) At "**700**" feet above the ground, begin a **LEFT** "**90**" degree CROSSWIND turn; What altitude is that?_____(20 pts)

11) With wings level, check your airspace and begin another **LEFT** "**90**" degree turn to the **LEFT** DOWNWIND

** 12) Your heading for the CROSSWIND leg is _____ (15 pts)
Your heading for the DOWNWIND leg is _____ (15 pts)

"You know what's an easy as pie rule of thumb to remember when it comes to rolling out from any turn? It's not in the books this way, but simply lead all your roll outs by 10 degrees before your target heading. There are more specific considerations, but for now, that'll make all your concentration brain waves work full time!"

13) Reduce power to about "**2300**" RPM at "**1000**" feet above the ground (AGL)

*"Well, lookie, lookie! I keep on saying that you should have about an "**800**" feet per minute climb rate on your Vertical Speed Indicator (VSI) and you sure do, don't you?!! Now pay attention as you get abeam the midfield of Aurora because then comes the next step. We will do what's standard, and that is depart out of the airport environment on a 45 degree 'I'm out of here!' heading!"*

Pattern Departure:

1) Hold the downwind course until midfield of Runway 18-36

**   2) Record the heading displayed on your DG_____(20 pts)
       Record the altitude you're passing_____(15 pts)

**   3) At midfield, turn **RIGHT** "**45**" degrees, maintaining the climb
       What will that heading be?_____(15 pts)

"You know, you could do 30 degree bank turns, but what's the rush? Simply make all your turns STANDARD RATE. You make a STANDARD RATE turn by keeping the wings on the little airplane, displayed on the TURN COORDINATOR, aligned with the "R" indicator. This way, you're right from the start practicing on smooth, minor movements, which will definitely help in the instrument environment. I remember once, flying a hop (flight in military terms) in the goo (clouds), when my brain (very small part of my head!) had me flying upside down (not good!) all the way through! Believe me, all corrections I made were anything but abrupt, and rightly so!!"

Level off:

1) Begin to level off when the altimeter reads "**2900**" feet
2) Maintain "**3000**" feet
3) Reduce power to about "**2250**" **[2450]** RPM

4) When settled, press "**P**" to pause the simulation
**   5) Record your:
       NAV 1 DME DIST_____(25 pts)
       HEADING_____(20 pts)
       RPM_____(20 pts)
       AIRSPEED_____(15 pts)
       GEAR_____(10 pts)
       FLAPS_____(10 pts)
6) Press "**P**" to continue the simulation

6

Course change #1:

"Can you see that airport in front of us or around in front? That just happens to be right about where your Number 1 VOR needle should center. So you see, when you're smart in this kind of environment, you have visual landmarks that you're relying on, and as a backup, use that VOR of yours. Why not? They are all tools to help you navigate from one place to another. If one breaks down, or you get confused, you have a map that still tells you what to do. That's called preparation!!!"

1) Watch your **NAV 1 CDI,** and when the needle is **centered,** start your **LEFT** turn to a heading of "**210**"

2) After you have rolled out, press "**P**" to pause the simulation

** 3) Record your:

      NAV 1 DME DIST_____(25 pts)
      ALTITUDE_____(20 pts)
      NAV 2 DME DIST_____(20 pts)

4) Press "**P**" to continue the simulation

5) Set power to about "**2300**" **[2500]** RPM and climb to "**4500**"ft

6) When level at "**4500**" feet, reduce power back to about "**2250**" **[2450]** RPM and set **NAV 1 OBS** to "**256**"

"Ah, I just wanted to see you do some climbing maneuvers while you were cruising en route to Bloomington-Normal. Plus you can see a bit more up here to help you get stabilized on exactly where you are, or where you want to be! But most importantly, it's so that you can be at your necessary VFR cruising altitude. For your westerly heading, the rule is even thousand plus 500 feet."

Course change #2:

1) Watch your **NAV 2 CDI,** and when the needle is one half dot **RIGHT** of center, start your **LEFT** turn to a heading of "**168**"

"Again, see how this equates to the city of Ottawa down there? I think you're beginning to see that when planning for these VFR (visual flight rules) flights, that there are almost always a wealth of ground points to draw from. There's the Illinois River big as life down there, huh??!!! Are you seeing the lesson gained from this specific flight? You sure are flying it well, so I think you must be!"

2) As a cross check, the **NAV 1 CDI** needle should almost be centered

3) Track inbound on the "**348**" radial ("168" heading in the upper window)

4) Tune **NAV 1** to "**108.2**" (BMI), and set "**210**" in the upper window

5) Press "**P**" to pause the simulation

** 6) Record your:

      NAV 1 DME DIST_____(25 pts)

      NAV 2 DME DIST_____(25 pts)

      AIRSPEED_____(20 pts)

      HEADING_____(20 pts)

7) Press "**P**" to continue the simulation

8) Reduce power to about "**2100**" [**2300**] RPM and descend at "**400**" feet per minute to "**3500**" feet

9) When level, return power to about "**2250**" [**2450**] RPM

"What? Me overload you?? Impossible! You're so far ahead of this airplane that I've had to personally go full power to get you back in the cockpit!!! But do remember, that to track inbound on a VOR radial, just keep the CDI needle centered by making minor heading changes to compensate for winds. What I mean by minor is that if you constantly drift to the right, the needle will be to the left. So chase the needle and make a left 20 degree correction. When the needle centers, take out half of that correction and then keep working it in that manner."

6

Course change #3:

1) Watch your **NAV 2 DME DIST**, as it reaches **"0.5"**, turn **RIGHT** to a heading of **"182"**

2) Cross check to see that the **NAV 1 CDI** needle should almost be centered

"Ah! Can you almost smell how close we are to our destination? If you look at your VFR sectional, we are now starting to fly on a low altitude airway called Victor 313 or V313. They are, so to speak, highways in the sky, mostly for instrument pilots. Well, be thinking about landing because it's not too far now, so press on!"

3) Set **NAV 2 OBS** to **"182"** in the upper window

4) Track outbound on the **"182"** radial that your **NAV 2 OBI** is displaying

5) Set **NAV 1 OBS** to **"240"** in the upper window

*"Look how well you're thinking ahead! That setting of **240** is in preparation for the 45 degree entry into Bloomington-Normal. As a matter of fact, you are so well ahead of the game, let's get the ATIS information on **135.35** to see which runway is active. I believe we've guessed it to be runway 11, right?"*

6) Tune **COM** to **"135.35"** (Bloomington-Normal ATIS)

"BLOOMINGTON-NORMAL AIRPORT, INFORMATION NOVEMBER, 1730 ZULU WEATHER, SKY CLEAR, VISIBILITY 40. TEMPERATURE 91, WIND 090 AT 10. ALTIMETER 29.95. LANDING AND DEPARTING RUNWAY 11. ADVISE ON INITIAL CONTACT YOU HAVE INFORMATION NOVEMBER."

"Well, how do you like that? Did we get Bingo on that one, or did we get Bingo on that one? We're setting this up perfectly. Watch that Number 1 needle now - pretty soon, we'll have that field in sight. I can see it in my mind's eye. But wait on calling tower until we get heading inbound, because there is no rush!"

7) Watch your **NAV 1 CDI,** and when the needle is one half dot **LEFT** of center, start a **RIGHT** turn to a heading of **"240"**
8) Start to roll out when you see **"232"** in the **DG** window
9) Maintain a heading of **"240"**

"If winds are the same as when we departed, then we have a strong crosswind with a little tailwind! Watch for drift on the approach. Look for the airport! You can just barely see its outline!"

Descent:

1) The airfield should now be in front of you plainly in sight.

*"Now's as good a time as any to call Tower on **124.6**, give our position and intentions (you do know them, don't you?), get down to traffic pattern altitude, and set up our cockpit for landing. Now remember, if I don't get scared, I'll give you my **'13MIKE'** hat! Take it away, El Pilot!"*

2) Tune **COM** on **"124.6"** (Bloomington-Normal Tower)

You:

"BLOOMINGTON-NORMAL TOWER, THIS IS CESSNA 13MIKE, ABOUT EIGHT MILES NORTHEAST OF THE FIELD, INBOUND ON A LEFT 45 FOR LANDING WITH NOVEMBER."

Bloomington-Normal Tower:

"13MIKE, CONTINUE INBOUND. REPORT WHEN AT FIVE MILES."

You:

"13MIKE WILL REPORT AT FIVE."

6

3) Set **ALTIMETER**, set **DG**, and check **FUEL**

4) Set the **DME** to "**NAV 1**"

5) When established inbound, reduce power to about "**1800**" [**2100**] RPM, descend and maintain "**1900**" feet and plan to arrive at altitude when the **NAV 1 DME DIST** equals "**5.0**"

You:

> **"BLOOMINGTON-NORMAL TOWER, 13MIKE IS AT FIVE MILES ON THE 45."**

Bloomington-Normal Tower:

> **"13MIKE, REPORT WHEN ABEAM THE TOWER."**

You:

> **"13MIKE."**

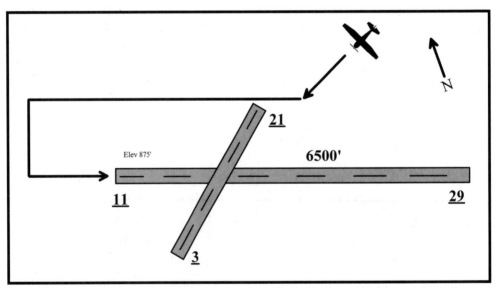

Figure 6.2. 45 degree entry for Left Downwind runway 11

Approach:

**   1) When abeam a point on the runway between the departure end of runway 11 and midfield, begin a **RIGHT** turn to the DOWNWIND leg. Heading _____(20 pts)

You:

"BLOOMINGTON-NORMAL TOWER, 13MIKE IS LEFT DOWNWIND ABEAM THE TOWER FOR LANDING."

Bloomington-Normal Tower:

"13MIKE, YOU'RE CLEARED TO LAND ON RUNWAY 11. YOUR TRAFFIC IS JUST NOW TURNING FROM LEFT BASE TO FINAL."

You:

"13MIKE IS LOOKING FOR TRAFFIC."

2) **CARB HEAT "ON"** and set **GEAR "DOWN"**

"Now don't forget to keep looking for that traffic. Don't get so busy in the cockpit that you forget your number one responsibility. Most collisions happen right here in the traffic pattern, and we do not want to contribute to that statistic! Do you see him? I do! Keep looking, you know about where he is - that's right! All right, tell tower you have him."

You:

"BLOOMINGTON-NORMAL TOWER, 13MIKE HAS TRAFFIC."

Bloomington-Normal Tower:

"13MIKE, CONTINUE TO LANDING."

3) Reduce power to about **"1500"** **[1800]** RPM
4) When you have slowed to **90 knots,** set **FLAPS** to **first notch**
5) When abeam the approach end of runway 11, begin a descent and maintain **400** ft per minute

"Okay! Now what's the standard law of Calfior while you're in the landing pattern? Repeat after me! **Adjust height with power, and airspeed with pitch.** *Hey, not bad! Keep it coming down. See if you can make this landing a stabilized ride down to the touchdown area with very little adjustment in nose or power."*

6

** 6) When the end of the runway is at your 5 o'clock position, turn **LEFT "90"** degrees to establish your BASE leg of the approach. Heading_____(20 pts)

7) Set **FLAPS** to **second notch** (20 degrees)

8) Press **"P"** to pause the simulator

** 9) Record your:

        AIRSPEED_____(25 pts)
        VSI_____(25 pts)
        ALTITUDE_____(20 pts)
        HEADING_____(20 pts)
        RPM_____(20 pts)
        CARB HEAT_____(10 pts)
        LIGHTS_____(10 pts)
        GEAR_____(10 pts)

10) Press **"P"** to continue the simulation

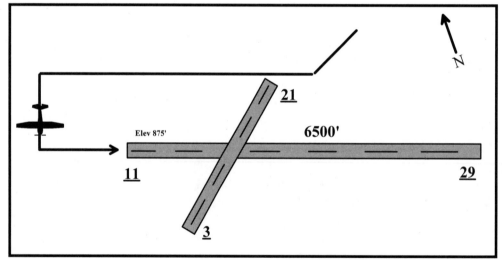

Figure 6.3. Left BASE preparing to turn FINAL for runway 11.

11) When runway 11 is at your 10 o'clock position, start a **"90"** degree **LEFT** turn to your **FINAL** leg of the approach

*"You're doing fine! I'm not scared, so your hat is still available! But be aggressive in lining up with runway 11. Don't just watch the slide to the side - **make** slight heading adjustments to compensate for winds, overshoots, or undershoots."*

    12) When established on the FINAL leg, set **FLAPS** to **third notch** (30 degrees). Airspeed should be **70 knots**

"I think you might just do it! You haven't changed anything other than flaps, from abeam your point of intended landing right to this position! It's been perfectly right down the slide in a 180 degree oblong turn. Sure is pretty when you see it! Here! Wear the hat for now, just in case you screw up and I have to take it back!!!!!!"

    13) When the altimeter displays "**1100**" feet, press "**P**" to pause the simulation

**   14) Record your:

        AIRSPEED_____(25 pts)
        VSI_____(20 pts)
        HEADING_____(20 pts)
        RPM_____(20 pts)
        FLAPS_____(15 pts)

    15) Press "**P**" to continue the simulation
    16) When you are 10 to 20 feet off the runway, reduce power to about "**1000**" RPM, and start to slowly pitch the nose of the aircraft up to slow your descent and establish a touchdown attitude

"You're good on airspeed - 60 knots is solid here! This is great! We're still sliding down the final tube, and I think you've got it with hardly any adjustments!"

    17) When you are five feet off the runway, hold the nose of the aircraft up and allow the airspeed to **SLOWLY** bleed off. Your aircraft will **settle** onto the runway while you follow the centerline

6

"As smooth as you were from abeam to this landing attitude, be that smooth with your power and nose. Put on your ballet slippers! You know what I mean?"

18) After touchdown, reduce power to **600 RPM**
19) Apply the brakes
20) Turn left and taxi off the active runway
21) When aircraft has stopped, set **CARB HEAT** to "OFF"
22) Set **FLAPS** to "0"

"Take a picture of that approach in your mind, and carry it with you all the days of your career! That was an exquisitely executed erudition of an enormously easy appearing end-around done landing factually and effectively!!! Keep the hat!!! Switch to Ground Control on 125.0, close our flight plan and taxi for a pop, before we continue on to Kankakee Airport."

23) Tune **COM** to "125.0" (Bloomington-Normal Ground)

You:

"BLOOMINGTON-NORMAL GROUND, CESSNA 13MIKE IS DOWN AND CLEAR OF RUNWAY 11 FOR TAXI TO THE RAMP. I'D ALSO LIKE TO CLOSE MY VFR FLIGHT PLAN AT THIS TIME."

Bloomington-Normal Ground:

"13MIKE, YOU ARE CLEARED TO THE RAMP. YOUR FLIGHT PLAN IS CLOSED."

** 24) Record the **TIME** _____(5 pts)

TOTAL POINTS POSSIBLE FOR THIS FLIGHT IS__**700**__

✈ Flight Scenario Seven

Bloomington-Normal to Kankakee

(Chicago Area - estimated flying time 50 minutes)

Wind! Wind! Wind! It's no wonder they call Chicago the Windy City! I don't believe I've seen an airplane cover as much ground sideways as yours did in the last flight. Well, tell Professor Calfior that Professor Miller said if he is not tired of flying sideways with you, then you can skip the "SETUP" section and proceed to the "PREFLIGHT" section as you continue on to Kankakee. If this is your first flight with "13MIKE", let me tell you how we do the setup. I will lead you through the initial setup phase of the flight simulator where you will set the aircraft type, winds, and position. I will show you how to save this setup so you may return to the Bloomington-Normal Airport without going through the initial setup steps. I will then turn you over to Professor Calfior who will take you through the PREFLIGHT of "13MIKE" to set your instruments, TAXI, and perform a RUN UP of the engine prior to takeoff. He will instruct you in the TAKEOFF, CLIMB OUT, LEVEL OFF, COURSE CHANGES, DESCENT, APPROACH, and LANDING procedures that make up the bulk of this scenario. Please listen to what Professor Calfior has to say about flying techniques. He is trying to help you obtain the best possible score.

FLIGHT PLAN -

This route of flight follows well established departure, climb, cruise, descent, and landing procedures. The procedures begin with a departure from runway 3 at Bloomington-Normal Airport with a climb out to 3500 feet. You will perform a right 45 degree upwind leg departure. You will go 10 nautical miles outside of the airport, and then proceed direct to the ROBERTS VOR. Upon crossing ROBERTS, proceed outbound on a magnetic course of 024, and overfly the Greater Kankakee Airport. Proceed outbound on a heading of 085 for 2 minutes, execute a course reversal, and continue inbound to a right 45 degree traffic pattern entry to land on runway 4. After filling out our flight plan in Appendix A, and calling the Flight Service Station (FSS) to file it, we need to turn to Appendix B and locate the sectional map for Chicago. Find Bloomington-Normal and Kankakee airports. Draw the above route on the map. Now answer these questions.

**   a) How many Victor Airways converge at Roberts VOR?

_____(15 pts)

**   b) What major road parallels your track from Roberts VOR to Kankakee? _____(15 pts)

**   c) What is the name of the private airstrip, on the right, halfway between Roberts and Kankakee? _____(15 pts)

SETUP

Aircraft:
1) Choose **"Cessna Skylane RG"**

Weather:
1) Set Surface winds **"DEPTH"** to **"1200"**
2) Set Surface winds **"DIR"** to **"020"**
3) Set Surface winds **"SPEED"** to **"7"**

4) Set Level 1 "**TOPS**" to "**8000**"
5) Set Level 1 "**BASE**" to "**1200**"
6) Set Level 1 "**DIR**" to "**070**"
7) Set Level 1 "**SPEED**" to "**20**"

Aircraft Position:
1) "**NORTH**" to "16594.2751" -- [N040° 28' 49.6857]
2) "**EAST**" to "16244.9086" -- [W088° 55' 00.1581]
3) "**ALTITUDE**" to "882" -- [0]
4) "**HEADING**" to "290"

note: At this point you may wish to save this setup for future use.

PREFLIGHT

note: Set **ZOOM** to "1.0"
Set **TIME** to "13:30"

"I'm getting too old to be climbing in and out of this cockpit all day long! Hey, what happened to our Lear jet? Man, if we had one of those, we could do these flights in five minute bursts, couldn't we? But then we'd miss out on all the fun a 182 RG has to offer like vibration, prop noise, clunking gear down noises and pure aesthetic looks! Before I start crying, let's get ATIS on 135.35. As a note, have a piece of paper out and actually copy down some of this stuff. I've had students who listened to ATIS quite impassively, then asked them what it said, and they didn't have a clue!"

7

Instruments:

1) Tune **COM** to "135.35" (ATIS)

"BLOOMINGTON-NORMAL AIRPORT, INFORMATION OSCAR, 1830 ZULU WEATHER, SKY CLEAR, VISIBILITY 40, TEMPERATURE 92, WIND 020 AT 7. ALTIMETER 29.94. RUNWAY 3 IS THE ACTIVE RUNWAY FOR ALL DEPARTURES AND ARRIVALS. VASI LIGHTS ARE OUT OF SERVICE FOR RUNWAY 3 UNTIL FURTHER NOTICE. ADVISE ON INITIAL CONTACT YOU HAVE INFORMATION OSCAR."

"There must have been a wind shift since the time an hour or so ago when we landed. I don't know if you've ever tried to take off on a runway which sported tailwinds, but I'd say don't even try it as an experiment! The takeoff runs get pretty long and on a short runway, can cause quite some anxiety! Let's go ahead and set up the instruments as we need them for this leg to Kankakee."

2) Set "**Altimeter**" and "**DG**"
3) Set **XPDR** to "**1200**" (VFR code)
4) Tune **NAV 1** to "**108.2**" (BMI)
5) Tune **NAV 2** to "**116.8**" (RBS)
6) Set the **DME** to "**NAV 1**" and "**DIST**"
7) Check **CARB HEAT** is "**OFF**"
8) Check **GEAR** "**DOWN**"
9) Turn **STROBE** "**ON**"
10) Check **LIGHTS** are "**OFF**"

"Yup, that's sure right! Ground Control is next for taxi."

11) Tune **COM** to "**121.65**" (Bloomington-Normal Ground)

You:

"BLOOMINGTON-NORMAL GROUND, THIS IS CESSNA 13MIKE AT THE RAMP, READY TO TAXI TO RUNWAY 3 WITH INFORMATION OSCAR."

Bloomington-Normal Ground:

**"CESSNA 13MIKE, MAKE A LEFT TURN AND TAXI TO
RUNWAY 3. YOU ARE CLEARED TO CROSS RUNWAY
11-29 AT TAXIWAY CHARLIE."**

TAXI -

*"Boy, oh boy! Runway 11 is to our left. Taxi straight ahead, there must
be taxiway Charlie right there before runway 3 - turn LEFT. Continue
to taxi, since they have already cleared us to cross runway 11-29, until
you arrive at the runup area for runway 3. Turn right and hold short of
it. Perform your runup."* See Figure 7.1.

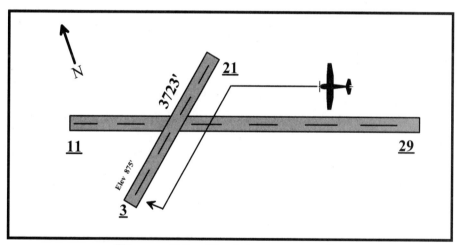

Figure 7.1. Taxi to runway 3.

7

RUN UP -

        1) Set brake (hold down to prevent aircraft from moving)
        2) Advance power to about "**1900**" RPM
**   3) Select CARB HEAT "**ON**", record RPM drop_____(5 pts)
        4) Select CARB HEAT "**OFF**"
**   5) Select "**LEFT**" Mag, record RPM drop_____(5 pts)

      6) Select "**BOTH**" Mags

**   7) Select "**RIGHT**" Mag, record RPM drop_____(5 pts)

      8) Select "**BOTH**" Mags

      9) Reduce power to **idle**

      10) Set **FLAPS** to **first notch** (10 degrees takeoff configuration)

"Wasn't there a song written about the Kankakee Choo-choo? Chattanooga? Is that right?!!! And I thought we were going some place real special!! What should we do next? Not Tower yet! Yeah, activate your flight plan - build that habit so that you never go airborne on a cross country without having filed and activated a flight plan."

You:

"BLOOMINGTON-NORMAL GROUND, 13MIKE WOULD LIKE TO ACTIVATE ITS VFR FLIGHT PLAN TO CHATTANOOGA - I MEAN, KANKAKEE AIRPORT AT THIS TIME!"

Bloomington-Normal Ground:

"13MIKE, YOUR FLIGHT PLAN TO KANKAKEE IS ACTIVATED AT THIS PRESENT TIME. HAVE A GREAT FLIGHT."

You:

"13MIKE, THANK YOU."

*"Talk about planting a thought seed!!!! Ground is probably laughing its head off now, so I'm glad we brightened up their day! Well, let's head up to the north then, and see what else we can learn about flying in visual conditions. You ready? Good! Tower is on **124.6,** and let's ask for an upwind departure."*

      11) Tune **COM** to "**124.6**" (Bloomington-Normal Tower)

You:

"BLOOMINGTON-NORMAL TOWER, CESSNA 13MIKE, READY FOR DEPARTURE RUNWAY 3. REQUEST AN UPWIND DEPARTURE."

Bloomington-Normal Tower:

> **"13MIKE, YOU ARE CLEARED FOR TAKEOFF. YOUR DISCRETION FOR DEPARTURE - NO INBOUNDS REPORTED."**

You:

> **"13MIKE, WE'LL CLEAR THE AREA AND EXIT UPWIND ON A RIGHT 45 TO ROBERTS. CLEARED FOR TAKEOFF."**

FLIGHT

Takeoff:

"If you were a beginning pilot, I'd say do all your checks first and then move out onto the runway. But we've done this several times in the past, so while moving, that's it, check that your flaps are in position, trimmed as desired for takeoff, oil temperature is in the green as well as the oil pressure. You're lined up perfectly on centerline - get that power on full and juice it!!!"

1) Record TIME _____
2) Release brakes and taxi onto runway 3
3) Advance power to **"FULL"**
4) Maintain centerline of runway
5) At **50 knots** airspeed lift nose wheel off runway
6) At **70 knots** ease back on the yoke to establish a 10 degree pitch up attitude
7) Maintain a climb **AIRSPEED** of **80 knots**
8) Raise **Gear** when there is no more runway to land on

"Check behind you to ensure that you are maintaining the runway centerline on the takeoff leg. Correct accordingly. You know, you should always be looking around. On maintaining runway heading, a method I advise is to pick a point in front of you when you're on the runway, and then after you're airborne a bit, still pointing at that reference, check behind you for alignment. Then you can correct that point."

7

** 9) At "**500**" feet above the ground, raise the **FLAPS** to "**0**"
What is your altitude? _____(20 pts)

** 10) At "**1000**" feet above the ground, make a "**45**" degree right
departure turn. What is that desired heading?_____(20 pts)

11) Reduce power to about "**2300**" RPM at "**1000**" feet above the
ground (AGL)

12) When wings are level, press "**P**" to pause the simulation

** 13) Record your:

> NAV 1 DME DIST_____(25 pts)
> ALTITUDE_____(20 pts)
> AIRSPEED_____(15 pts)
> VSI_____(15 pts)
> GEAR_____(10 pts)
> FLAPS_____(10 pts)

14) Press "**P**" to continue the simulation

Climb out & Level off:

1) Continue your climb to "**3500**" feet

2) Begin to level off when the altimeter reads "**3400**" feet

3) Maintain "**3500**" feet, set power to about "**2200**" [**2400**] RPM

4) Maintain the 45 degree departure course until you see "**10.0**"
on the **NAV 1 DME DIST**

To ROBERTS VOR:

*"Now I'm interested in working with you on another concept of the VOR.
And that is, rather than dialing in a predetermined heading on the
VOR, let's see what heading will bring us direct to Roberts VOR! You
know that when you are right on a desired radial, the CDI needle is
centered, and you correct to keep it centered. Since our Number 2 VOR
is already on Roberts VOR frequency, let's see what centers the needle.
Two headings will center the needle - one is 'TO' and the other is
'FROM'. We want to go **to** Roberts VOR."*

1) Set the **NAV 2 OBS** to whatever upper window heading that
will give you a "**TO**" with the needle being centered

2) Turn to the course shown in the upper window

3) When wings are level, press "**P**" to pause the simulation

** 4) Record your:

Ground speed from NAV 2_____(20 pts)

NAV 2 DME DIST_____(25 pts)

NAV 2 COURSE with centered needle_____(25 pts)

Airspeed_____(20 pts)

Estimated time en route from present

position to ROBERTS VOR_____(20 pts)

5) Press "**P**" to continue the simulation

6) Track inbound on your centered needle

"See! Can anything get more exciting than this!!! Let me reword that! Can anything worthwhile get more exciting ... never mind! Now you still apply the basic VOR principles of tracking. For instance, the winds at altitude are doing what to you? I'd say that you've got a correction coming and the needle is showing you that, isn't it? So offset by 20 degrees, wait for the needle to center, and then go back half that correction."

7) Tune **NAV 1** to "111.6" (IKK) and set "**024**" in the upper window

Course change #1:

1) Watch your **NAV 2 DME DIST** and as it reaches "**0.4**", turn left to a heading of "**024**"

2) Cross check to see that the **NAV 1 CDI** needle should almost be centered

"Remember, the cruise winds are from '070' at 20 knots. The 024 course will get you to Greater Kankakee airport directly with no winds. Could that mean that we might need to think about a crab in order to fly our desired track to the airport? Look at the ground! You can almost see as well as feel the left lateral movement we are making!"

7

**   3) From the above, what might be a **good heading** to go to?
        _____ (20 pts)

4) Fly that heading and visually scan outside for possible traffic

Descent:

*"Greater Kankakee Airport is set up somewhat differently than what you're used to seeing. There is no ATIS, since there is only a UNICOM facility there. To get the local altimeter setting, you must talk to Kankakee Radio, which is on frequency **122.2**. Ultimately, we still need to advise UNICOM of our position and intentions, but for now, let's just get the altimeter setting."*

1) When **NAV 2 DME** reads "**8.0**", tune **COM** to "**122.2**"

You:

"KANKAKEE RADIO, CESSNA 13MIKE, SAY PRESENT ALTIMETER SETTING PLEASE."

Kankakee Radio:

"CESSNA 13MIKE, LOCAL KANKAKEE ALTIMETER SETTING IS 29.99."

2) Set **ALTIMETER**, set **DG**, and check **FUEL**
3) Set **CARB HEAT** to "**ON**"

4) Press "**P**" to pause the simulation
**   5) Record your:
        NAV 1 DME DIST_____(25 pts)
        ALTITUDE_____(20 pts)
        HEADING_____(20 pts)
        AIRSPEED_____(15 pts)
6) Press "**P**" to continue the simulation

*"I'd say that definitely fits the description on the VFR sectional of the city of Kankakee! The airport is melted somewhere on its southern border by the railroad tracks, so we know we're close. Let's go and contact Kankakee UNICOM on **123.0** and see what earthshaking news they can dish out to us!"*

7) Tune **COM** to "**123.0**" (Kankakee UNICOM)

You:

"KANKAKEE UNICOM, THIS IS CESSNA 13MIKE ABOUT TEN MILES SOUTHWEST OF THE FIELD AT 3500 FEET, INBOUND FOR LANDING. REQUEST LANDING ADVISORY."

Kankakee UNICOM:

"CESSNA 13MIKE, WINDS ARE OUT OF THE NORTHEAST AT 5 TO 10 KNOTS, RUNWAY 4 IS THE ACTIVE RUNWAY AND NO REPORTED TRAFFIC OTHER THAN YOU INBOUND."

You:

"13MIKE WILL MANEUVER TO THE NORTHEAST AND ENTER ON A RIGHT 45 DEGREE ENTRY FOR A FULL STOP ON RUNWAY 4. WILL REPORT A THREE MILE 45."

"What we are doing now is not exactly standard procedure other than setting up for a 45 degree entry to the active runway. We could just circle to our right and come in on the 45, but I'd like you to see an instrument style sort of course reversal which will challenge your practical application skills! And since nobody is around, we've got the whole airspace to flop around in!! That's the beauty of uncontrolled fields - look at all the things you can get away with!!!!! As long as safety isn't compromised, right?"

8) When the general airport area is in sight, reduce power to about "**2000**" **[2200]** RPM
9) Descend to "**2300**" feet

10) At "**2300**" feet, increase power to about "**2200**" [**2400**] RPM

"This starts your approach descent to Greater Kankakee airport. We'll overfly the field so we can have a good starting point. Then we'll never lose visual of it, but like I said, the practice procedure will be good."

11) When overhead the field, turn right to a heading of "**085**"
12) Start timing on a heading of "**085**" for **2 minutes**

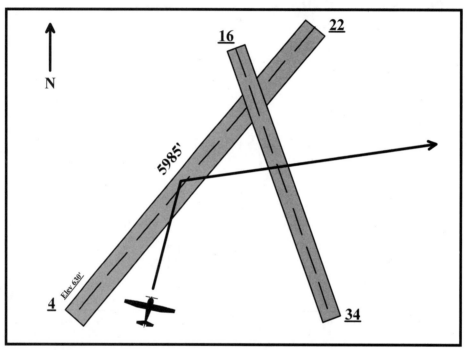

Figure 7.2.   Fly over of runway 4 and RIGHT turn to 085

*"Now, as you can see, we are proceeding outbound away from runway 4 on a 45 degree angle. This is a good track, but it's going in the wrong direction. I want you to execute what is called in the instrument environment a 'procedure turn', also called an **80-260** course reversal. Wait until two minutes go by and then execute it."*

Traffic pattern entry:

    1) At the end of 2 minutes, turn **RIGHT** for **80** degrees of heading change

**   2) Heading _____ (20 pts)

    3) At the completion of 80 degrees of turn, smoothly reverse the turn to the **LEFT** for **260** degrees of heading change

**   4) Heading _____ (20 pts)

"This procedure is actually accomplished in the instrument environment with a standard rate turn. Do you see how it can now be applied to reversing a course to a desired track? And the standard rate-ness of the turn is vital because of the timing that it entails. But I won't go into that now. Can you draw a picture in your mind and tell me where we'll be at the end of this left 260 degree turn?"

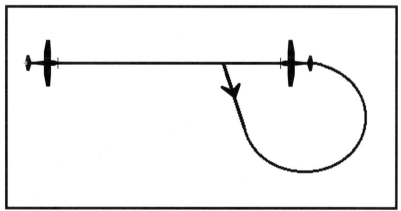

Figure 7.3. A right "**80-260**" degree course

5) When the reversal is complete, press **"P"** to pause the simulation

6) Record your:

NAV 1 DME DIST_____(25 pts)

ALTITUDE_____(20 pts)

RIGHT DOWNWIND HEADING_____(20 pts)

CARB HEAT_____(10 pts)

CURRENT HEADING_____(10 pts)

7) Press **"P"** to continue the simulation

All right! Now back to where we left off. Look! There's K-Mart, the home of the blue light special again!!!! You see, we simply reversed ourselves and are now revisiting the 45 degree track, but now it's towards runway 4 of Greater Kankakee Airport! This could even be put into the category of cooler than the VOR needle centering and you turning to that heading! Slow down, my racing heart, slow down!!!!!"

Approach:

1) Approach the runway at a **"45"** degree angle. After completion of the 80-260 maneuver, descend to **"1600"** feet

2) Reduce power to about **"1400" [1700]** RPM

"Remember that you told them you'd call at the three mile 45, which is about where you are at right now! We are also beginning our approach descent into the landing pattern."

You:

"KANKAKEE TRAFFIC, CESSNA 13MIKE IS ON A THREE MILE RIGHT 45 FOR RUNWAY 4, FULL STOP."

3) When you are about **one mile** from the runway, make a **LEFT** turn to enter the DOWNWIND leg of the approach

"Hey, would you set your gams on that rectangular slab of asphalt! I just saw 'West Side Story', so the New York lingo slips in every once in a while! Translated, I said, you should be able to see the runway out your right side window as you are flying parallel to it!"

4) Select **GEAR "DOWN"**
5) When you have slowed to **90 knots,** set **FLAPS** to **first notch**

"You are flying around in an uncontrolled airport, where anybody can come in at will, not see you, run right into you, stall, turn upside down, and both meet the ground at quite a rapid rate! Since I'm not interested in that story, let's tell traffic, whoever they are or will be, that we are right downwind, right base, right final (?), et cetera, et cetera, et cetera! The night before last, I saw 'The King and I'!!!"

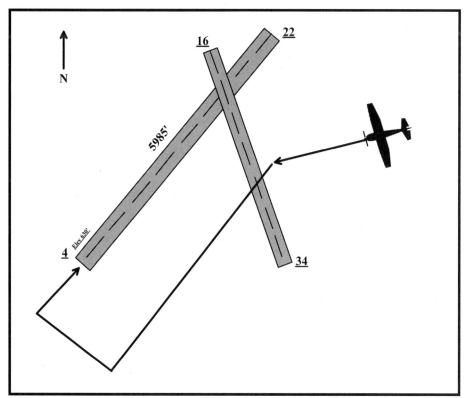

Figure 7.4 45 entry for RIGHT DOWNWIND

7

You:

> **"KANKAKEE TRAFFIC, CESSNA 13MIKE IS RIGHT DOWNWIND FOR RUNWAY 4, FULL STOP."**

> 6) Abeam the approach end of runway 4, begin your descent to landing
> 7) Try and maintain a **400** ft per minute descent

"Quiz time!!! You ready??!"

**   8) Adjust height with_____(20 pts)
      9) Adjust airspeed with_____(20 pts)

> 10) When the end of the runway is at your 5 o'clock position, turn **RIGHT "90"** degrees to establish your BASE leg of the approach
> 11) Set **FLAPS** to **second notch** (20 degrees)

> 12) Press **"P"** to pause the simulation

**   13) Record your:
          AIRSPEED_____(25 pts)
          ALTITUDE_____(25 pts)
          RPM_____(20 pts)
          HEADING_____(20 pts)
          VSI_____(15 pts)
          CARB HEAT_____(15 pts)
          GEAR_____(10 pts)
   14) Press **"P"** to continue the simulation

You:

> **"KANKAKEE TRAFFIC, CESSNA 13MIKE IS ON RIGHT BASE FOR RUNWAY 4, FULL STOP."**

> 15) When runway 4 is at your 2 o'clock position, start a **"90"** degree **RIGHT** turn to your **FINAL** leg of the approach

"You got to love me while we're in the airplane, because I can pull the mixture any time, raise the flaps inappropriately, sing a rendition of 'Oklahoma' which I saw three nights ago, or anything!! But I'd suggest that you line up on runway 4 and not the taxiway!!! Make slight heading adjustments to compensate for winds, overshoots, or undershoots."

16) When on the FINAL approach, set **FLAPS** to **third notch**

You:

"KANKAKEE TRAFFIC, CESSNA 13MIKE IS ON FINAL FOR RUNWAY 4, FULL STOP."

17) Airspeed should be **70 knots**

"If you're low, add power - if you're high, reduce power - if you're low in speed, lower nose - if you're high in speed, raise nose. Then fine tune everything else to hold that perfect picture of the runway threshold on your windscreen. WOW!!!! You're right on the mark! Capture that picture and take it with you to the numbers!!!"

18) When the Altimeter displays "**800**" feet, press "**P**" to pause the simulation
19) Record your:
> AIRSPEED_____(20 pts)
> VSI_____(20 pts)
> HEADING_____(15 pts)
> RPM_____(15 pts)
> FLAPS_____(10 pts)

20) Press "**P**" to continue the simulation

21) When you are 10 feet off the runway, reduce power to about "**1000**" RPM and start to slowly pitch the nose of the aircraft up to slow your descent and establish a touchdown attitude

*"WATCH YOUR **AIRSPEED**! 60 - 60 - 60 - 60!!! Hike!! Don't get stally on me! Don't let your airspeed drop below **60 knots**."*

7

22) When you are five feet off the runway, hold the nose of the aircraft up and allow the airspeed to **SLOWLY** bleed off. Your aircraft will **settle** onto the runway while you follow the centerline

"Your peripheral vision can track the sides of the runway and help you to gently **settle** *13MIKE onto the runway smoothly, and appearance wise, effortlessly. Of course, we know it takes lots of work, but spectators don't."*

23) After touchdown, reduce power to **600 RPM**
24) Apply the brakes
25) Turn right and taxi off the active runway
26) When aircraft has stopped, set **CARB HEAT** to "OFF"
27) Set **FLAPS** to "0"

"You have flown this leg like a champ!!! And that's with all kinds of new procedures learned, and you never even missed a beat! Let traffic know we're clear of the active and we'll get a drink, talk about what you learned, and close this flight plan over the phone. When I was a rich man - yabba dabba dooba - doobie - dum!!! Sorry, that's from 'Fiddler On The Roof'!"

You:

"KANKAKEE TRAFFIC, CESSNA 13MIKE IS DOWN AND CLEAR OF THE ACTIVE. TAXIING TO THE SHACK."

**   28) Record the **TIME**_____(5 pts)

TOTAL POINTS POSSIBLE FOR THIS FLIGHT IS__**785**__

✈ Flight Scenario Eight

Kankakee to Chicago Meigs Field

(Chicago Area - estimated flying time 30 minutes)

Professor Miller here! Kankakee? Kankakee? Isn't there a song about Kankakee? I always wondered where that city was. Well, now we all know, don't we? The fourth and last flight of this series departs Greater Kankakee Airport and arrives at Chicago Meigs Field along the southern shoreline of Lake Michigan. It may be flown as the last flight of this series or as a complete self contained flight. If you are continuing on with Professor Calfior, you may skip the "SETUP" section. If this is your first flight with "13MIKE", let me tell you how we do the setup. I will lead you through the initial setup phase of the flight simulator where you will set the aircraft type, winds, and position. I will show you how to save this setup so you may return to the Kankakee Airport without going through the initial setup steps. I will then turn you over to Professor Calfior who will take you through the PREFLIGHT of "13MIKE" to set your instruments, TAXI, and perform a RUN UP of the engine prior to takeoff. He will instruct you in the TAKEOFF, CLIMB OUT, LEVEL OFF, COURSE CHANGES, DESCENT, APPROACH, and LANDING procedures that make up the bulk of this scenario. Please listen to what Professor Calfior has to say about flying techniques. He is trying to help you obtain the best possible score.

8

FLIGHT PLAN -

The route of flight follows well established departure, climb, cruise, descent, and landing procedures. The procedures begin with a departure from runway 34 at Greater Kankakee Airport, with a climb out to 3500 feet. You will be following Interstate 57 until abeam Sanger Field, and then proceed direct to Chicago Heights VOR. You will then execute the **Shore Visual Runway 36** approach into Chicago Meigs Field. After filling out our flight plan in Appendix A, and calling the Flight Service Station (FSS) to file it, we need to turn to Appendix B and locate the sectional map for Chicago. Find Kankakee Airport and Chicago Meigs Field. Draw the above route on the map. Now answer these questions.

** a) About a minute or two prior to reaching abeam Sanger Field, you bypass a tower whose elevation is how many feet mean sea level (MSL)?_____(15 pts)

** b) What airport, to the east, should you see as you proceed to Meigs Field from Chicago Heights?_____ (15 pts)

** c) What is the name of the Airport Radar Service Area (ARSA) that's to your left as you fly inbound to Meigs Field?_____(15 pts)

SETUP

Aircraft:
    1) Choose **"Cessna Skylane RG"**

Weather:
    1) Set Surface winds **"DEPTH"** to **"1200"**
    2) Set Surface winds **"DIR"** to **"020"**
    3) Set Surface winds **"SPEED"** to **"7"**
    4) Set Level 1 **"TOPS"** to **"8000"**
    5) Set Level 1 **"BASE"** to **"1200"**

6) Set Level 1 "**DIR**" to "070"

~~~ "**SPEED**" to "20"

6847.3909" -- [N041° 04' 24.0444]

97.2339" -- [W087° 50' 48.2350]

o "627" -- [0]

"130"

hay wish to save this setup for future use.

REFLIGHT

M to "1.0"

to "15:00"

retty this airport was when we came in? The
picturesque and broad winding right up to our
w it for a while as we depart, just in case you
he way in. Thanks, Professor Miller, for your
th my student - it was superb as ever! I'm
Califor, not California, not Cauliflower, but the
ht with the letters! Sad to say, we have no ATIS
's give a jingle to UNICOM on **123.0** *for some*

to "**123.0**" (Kankakee UNICOM)

OM, CESSNA 13MIKE IS AT THE RAMP,
TO TAXI. COULD YOU GIVE US SOME
ON WINDS, RUNWAY IN USE, AND
TING, PLEASE?"

8

Kankakee UNICOM:

> **"13MIKE, WINDS ARE VARIABLE FROM THE NORTHWEST TO THE NORTHEAST AT 5 TO 10 KNOTS, YOUR CHOICE OF RUNWAYS FOR TAKEOFF, EITHER 34 OR 4, ALTIMETER SETTING 30.01."**

"So we can follow the river a bit, let's advise them that we'll head for runway 34 when we're ready to taxi. It'll be a straight out departure. Get your cross country materials organized in this cockpit, and set up the navigation instruments. Gee, this'll be our last leg together in Chicago, won't it? I fly out to San Francisco tomorrow for another spectacular series of flights - you can come if you like!"

2) Set "**Altimeter**" and "**DG**"
3) Set **XPDR** to "**1200**" (VFR code)
4) Tune **NAV 1** to "**114.2**" (CGT)
5) Set **NAV 1 OBS** to acquire a centered needle and a **'TO'** indication
6) Tune **NAV 2** to "**114.2**" (CGT)
7) Set **NAV 2 OBS** to "**356**" in the upper window
8) Set the **DME** to "**NAV 1**" and "**DIST**"
9) Check **CARB HEAT** is "**OFF**" and **GEAR** "**DOWN**"
10) Turn **STROBE** "**ON**" and **LIGHTS** are "**OFF**"

You:

> **"KANKAKEE UNICOM, 13MIKE WILL BE TAXIING TO RUNWAY 34 FOR DEPARTURE. THANKS FOR YOUR HOSPITALITY."**

Kankakee UNICOM:

> **"13MIKE, YOU'RE WELCOME. ENJOYED YOUR COMPANY. HAVE A GOOD FLIGHT UP NORTH."**

TAXI -

"Runway 4 is at your back. So make a right turn and taxi along the taxiway to the Terminal. Make a left turn at the Terminal and taxi along the taxiway to the runup area of runway 34. We will perform our runup there. I can hardly wait to get airborne, because this is going to be such a pretty flight all the way through!" See Figure 8.1

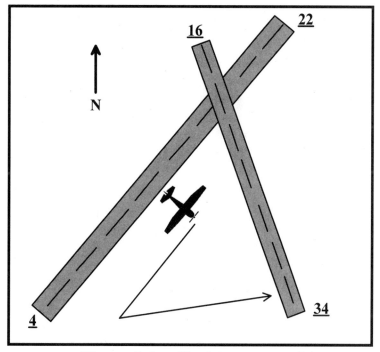

Figure 8.1.   Taxi to runway 34

RUN UP -

"Well, that gave us a little taxi tour of the south side of the airport, didn't it? Did you see that jackrabbit scoot by our right side as we turned left at the Terminal? I didn't think the Chicago area had jackrabbits! Plenty of them where I come from, Arizona! Well, who cares! Before we get airborne, make sure the engine is operating up to snuff and finish off the pretake-off checklist."

8

1) Set brake (hold down to prevent aircraft from moving)

  2) Advance power to about "**1700**" RPM

** 3) Select CARB HEAT "**ON**", record RPM drop_____(5 pts)

  4) Select CARB HEAT "**OFF**"

** 5) Select "**LEFT**" Mag, record RPM drop_____(5 pts)

  6) Select "**BOTH**" Mags

** 7) Select "**RIGHT**" Mag, record RPM drop_____(5 pts)

  8) Select "**BOTH**" Mags

  9) Reduce power to **idle** and ensure **FLAPS** are up

*"Yeah, you're right! I just want to see you do this takeoff without any flaps - it's not so outlandish that it isn't done! As a matter of fact, we've been using 10 degrees flaps, and that's what the pilot operating handbook advises for a short or soft field takeoff. I wanted to see you do one without flaps, so I will! Now, another thing! There is a Flight Service Station on this field, as you know, and I want you to open your flight plan with them on frequency **122.1**. That's a standard frequency for all FSSs, so you can't go wrong jumping on that one! Go ahead!"*

  10) Tune **COM** to "**122.1**" (Kankakee Radio)

You:

"KANKAKEE RADIO, CESSNA 13MIKE WOULD LIKE TO ACTIVATE ITS VFR FLIGHT PLAN TO CHICAGO MEIGS FIELD RIGHT NOW."

Kankakee Radio:

"CESSNA 13MIKE, YOUR FLIGHT PLAN IS ACTIVATED AS OF 8 MINUTES PAST THE HOUR. GOOD DAY."

"It's so important to do all this prep work before actually getting airborne. Are you beginning to see that? Missing most any of our checklist items could cause quite a stir for you, the pilot, if you're not faithful in the performance of your pretake-off responsibilities. That's why I harp on you to stay with it, focused and serious on setting up your airplane each and every flight. But enough is enough, for crying out loud! Get me airborne before I sprout wings and fly without this contraption! Let traffic know what we plan to do."

You:

> **"KANKAKEE TRAFFIC, CESSNA 13MIKE IS ROLLING ONTO THE ACTIVE, RUNWAY 34, FOR A STRAIGHT OUT DEPARTURE TO THE NORTH."**

FLIGHT

Takeoff:

"Are we airborne yet? I've got get-air-itis, rather than get-home-itis! All right, flaps are up for this takeoff, enough fuel to get to Meigs, trimmed to perfection, and both oil temperature and pressure are happy figures! Hup, two, three, four - centerline this thing and let's see the river!"

1) Record TIME _____
2) Release brakes and taxi onto runway 34
3) Advance power to **"FULL"**
4) Maintain centerline of runway
5) At **50 knots** airspeed lift nose wheel off runway
6) At **70 knots** ease back on the yoke to establish a 10 degree pitch up attitude, maintain a climb **AIRSPEED** of **80** knots
7) Raise **Gear** when there is no more runway to land on
8) At **"500"** feet above the ground (AGL), increase climb **AIRSPEED** to **90** knots
9) Reduce power to about **"2300"** RPM at **"1000"** feet AGL

*"With this lower nose attitude climb schedule, you should be seeing approximately a **"900 to 950"** feet per minute climb rate on your Vertical Speed Indicator (VSI). Oh, look at the Kankakee River!"*

Climb out:

1) Maintain runway heading to **"1200"** feet, then follow Interstate **57** northbound

8

"Just as a reminder, since I feel like I've neglected to say this enough, all turns should be STANDARD RATE. You make a STANDARD RATE turn by keeping the wings on the little airplane displayed on the TURN COORDINATOR aligned with the "L" indicator in this case. Now, if you were doing an aileron roll, you wouldn't be using your turn coordinator! Wouldn't that be a blast just to try it once in this airplane? Go ahead - no, don't! Oh, what the heck, do it! No, let's do it in a simulator first!

Level off:

1) Begin to level off when the altimeter reads "**3400**" feet
2) Maintain "**3500**" feet, set power to about "**2150**" **[2350]** RPM

"Like I said, isn't the scenery here gorgeous? Say bye to the river off to the left! Well, we're looking for Sanger Field as our first official checkpoint, though there's plenty of others out here. So enjoy the leisure, but the pace will certainly pick up as we near Chicago Proper. Boy, has this been a good day or what!!!!?"

Course change:

1) When **abeam Sanger Field**, proceed direct to **Chicago Heights VOR**
2) Center the **NAV 1 CDI** needle with a **'TO'** indication
3) Turn to that heading
4) When established inbound, press "**P**" to pause the simulation
** 5) Record your:
> GROUND SPEED_____(20 pts)
> NAV 1 DME DIST_____(25 pts)
> ALTITUDE_____(20 pts)
> CENTERED NAV 1 CDI HEADING_____(25 pts)
> AIRSPEED_____(15 pts)
> VSI_____(15 pts)

6) Press "**P**" to continue the simulation

"Do you catch that smell? The combination of aviation fuel and Lake Michigan! Oh, sweet heaven!!! Now be aware of your environment at all times. You have the Chicago TCA, but we will be descending so that it doesn't affect us. We will be brushing by the ARSA whose floor is 1900 feet, but we'll even be below that! Did you notice all this when you planned this flight? It's like putting a puzzle together and seeing it all accomplished as you fly - that's the fun of flying these cross countries! Well, it's time to go lower!"

Descent:

> 1) When **NAV 1 DME DIST** reads "**0.4**", then commence your turn to fly the **Shore Visual Rwy 36** into Chicago Meigs Field

*"Now we actually will be flying the **Shore Visual Rwy 36** approach into Chicago Meigs Field. We're not telling anybody that this is what we're doing - it's just for you to see how a visual approach is actually accomplished when coming from the instrument environment. You could say we're simulating it, but it'll be a straight in approach as far as Meigs Tower is concerned. So that turn is to a course of "356" as we've got set in on our NAV 2 VOR."*

> 2) Transition to your **NAV 2** display
> 3) When established outbound, reduce power to about "**1900**" [**2100**] RPM, descend and maintain "**1800**" feet

"Let's see you hold a 500 feet per minute rate of descent on this slide into Home Plate until you reach 1800 feet. While you're losing altitude, go get us some ATIS for supper!"

> 4) Tune **COM** to "**127.35**". (Meigs ATIS)

"CHICAGO MEIGS FIELD, INFORMATION YANKEE, 2000 ZULU WEATHER, SKY CLEAR, VISIBILITY 25 WITH HAZE. TEMPERATURE 79, WIND 020 AT 7. ALTIMETER 29.99. LANDING AND DEPARTING RUNWAY 36. ADVISE ON INITIAL CONTACT YOU HAVE INFORMATION YANKEE."

8

5) Set **ALTIMETER**, set **DG**, and check **FUEL**

"Isn't that peachy-keen? Runway 36, just as if we ordered it from a restaurant! Being that this is a busy airport, we need to call Tower early and tell them our intention to proceed straight in. Then maybe they'll coordinate us in between any traffic that's in the pattern, or other arrivals. I'd say we're about what - 12 miles or so from the field? Tower is on 121.3."

6) Tune **COM** to "**121.3**". (Meigs Tower)

You:

"CHICAGO MEIGS TOWER, CESSNA 13MIKE IS 12 MILES SOUTH OF THE FIELD, INBOUND FOR LANDING WITH YANKEE. WOULD LIKE TO REQUEST A STRAIGHT IN TO A FULL STOP, RUNWAY 36."

Meigs Tower:

"CESSNA 13MIKE, ADVISE WHEN YOU ARE ON A FIVE MILE INITIAL. MAINTAIN AT OR BELOW 1900 FEET TO AVERT SOUTHEAST PORTION OF CHICAGO MIDWAY ARSA."

You:

"13MIKE WILL REPORT AT FIVE MILES. PASSING 2600 FOR 1800 FEET."

7) Follow alongside Interstate **94** until you arrive abeam the **south shore** of Lake Michigan
8) When abeam **south shore,** press "**P**" to pause the simulation
** 9) Record your:

NAV 2 DME DIST_____(25 pts)
HEADING_____(20 pts)
ALTITUDE_____(20 pts)
AIRSPEED_____(15 pts)
VSI_____(15 pts)

10) Press "**P**" to continue the simulation

11) At "**1800**" feet, set your power to about "**1900**" **[2100]** RPM
and follow the shoreline inbound to Chicago Meigs Field

12) When the **NAV 2 DME DIST** reads "**15.5**":

*"Right now, from the looks of it, it's about as good a five mile initial as
you're going to get. You know what to do!"*

You:

**"MEIGS TOWER, 13MIKE IS AT A FIVE MILE INITIAL FOR
STRAIGHT IN TO 36."**

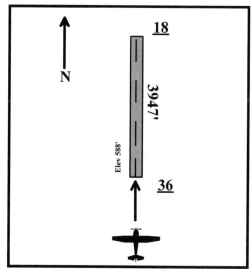

Figure 8.2.   Straight in for runway 36

Meigs Tower:

**"13MIKE, CONTINUE APPROACH.   YOUR LANDING
TRAFFIC IS COMMENCING A TURN FROM DOWNWIND
TO RIGHT BASE, AND ANOTHER IS ON A ONE MILE
FINAL. REPORT WHEN TRAFFIC IS IN SIGHT."**

*"I've got both of them. Do you? Yeah, pretty easy to spot that base turn,
when it's mirrored by the water, isn't it? All right, let them know."*

You:

    "MEIGS TOWER, 13MIKE HAS ITS TRAFFIC."

Meigs Tower:

    "13MIKE, YOU ARE CLEARED TO LAND ON RUNWAY 36. WILL YOU BE NEEDING FUEL?"

You:

    "13MIKE, THAT'S AFFIRMATIVE."

Approach:

    1) **CARB HEAT "ON"** and **GEAR "DOWN"**
    2) Reduce power to about **"1500" [1800]** RPM
    3) Correct to the left to line up on Runway 36
    4) When you have slowed to **90 knots,** set **FLAPS** to **first notch**

*"This is our last landing approach together - try a **"400"** feet per minute descent rate. It looks pretty neat, doesn't it? There's that guy on short final. Our other traffic is stepped up above him just turning from base to final, and then there's us overseeing it all! Lake Michigan is on the right, and there's Chicago Midway over our left shoulder! O'Hare is there left of our final approach course. This place is better than any movie!"*

    5) Set **FLAPS** to **second notch** when about two miles from the approach end. (18.5 DME)

*"Now this is a visual thing. What does **TWO** miles look like? The runway length is about 3/4 of a mile, so fold it over toward you and then add some. Right about here will do it! That's a visual trick you can pull on yourself, and it works consistently! Watch your descent. Try and maintain the same runway aspect as you continue your descent. Don't let that runway end rise or fall."*

6) When "**ONE**" mile from the approach end (19.5 DME), set **FLAPS** to **third notch**, airspeed should be **70** knots

"Adjust height with power, and airspeed with pitch - don't oscillate erratically on me! It's looking good, but trim up your stability."

7) Press "**P**" to pause the simulation

**   8) Record your:

AIRSPEED	_____	(25 pts)
VSI	_____	(20 pts)
HEADING	_____	(15 pts)
RPM	_____	(15 pts)
FLAPS	_____	(10 pts)
GEAR	_____	(10 pts)

9) Press "**P**" to continue the simulation

10) When you are 10 to 20 feet off the runway, reduce power to about "**1000**" RPM, and start to slowly pitch the nose of the aircraft up to slow your descent and establish a touchdown attitude

*"WATCH YOUR **AIRSPEED**! Be careful not to stall the aircraft. Just hold that attitude so that your runway perspective doesn't move. Get that landing attitude now - don't overcorrect and get fast on me. Shoot for that attitude! That's it! That's it! Now hold it! Never get below **60** knots."*

11) When you are five feet off the runway, hold the nose of the aircraft up and allow the airspeed to **SLOWLY** bleed off. Your aircraft will settle onto the runway while you follow the centerline

"Don't be impatient! Let the aircraft settle onto the runway slowly. Respond with your controls positively, yet gently!"

12) After touchdown, reduce power to **600 RPM**
13) Apply the brakes
14) Turn left and taxi off the active runway
15) When aircraft has stopped, set **CARB HEAT** to "**OFF**"

8

16) Set **FLAPS** to "**0**"

*"Chicago Meigs Field - the airport on the shore! You know, I'd bet you that if Microsoft ever made this airport into a default setting, it'd sell millions of copies of its Flight Simulator program! Let's switch to Ground Control on **121.8** and get our taxi clearance. There's the fuel facility, so we'll head there since they asked. Close out your flight plan too!"*

17) Tune **COM** to "**121.8**" (Meigs Ground)

You:

"CHICAGO MEIGS GROUND, CESSNA 13MIKE IS DOWN AND CLEAR OF RUNWAY 36. WOULD LIKE TO TAXI TO THE FUEL FACILITY."

Meigs Ground:

"CESSNA 13MIKE, TAXI TO THE FUEL FACILITY. FOLLOW THE YELLOW AND RED COURTESY TRUCK."

You:

"MEIGS GROUND, 13MIKE WOULD LIKE TO CLOSE ITS VFR FLIGHT PLAN ALSO."

Meigs Ground:

"FLIGHT PLAN CLOSED. ENJOY CHICAGO, 13MIKE!"

18) Taxi to the refueling pit next to the Tower
19) Shut down the engine

** 20) Record the **TIME**_____(5 pts)

TOTAL POINTS POSSIBLE FOR THIS FLIGHT__375__

✈ Flight Scenario Nine

Salinas to San Jose

(San Francisco Area - estimated flying time 45 minutes)

Flight Series Three. You must be a hot pilot by now! Well, we'll see how good your pilotage is with this flight. Professor Miller here, for the start of this two flight adventure. This flight will begin at Salinas Airport, which is south of San Francisco, and fly north to land at San Jose International. Sounds simple, huh? I will lead you through the initial setup phase of the flight simulator where you will set the aircraft type, winds, and position. I will show you how to save this setup so you may return to the Salinas Airport without going through the initial setup steps. I will then turn you over to Professor Calfior who will take you through the PREFLIGHT to set your instruments, TAXI, and perform a RUN UP of the engine prior to takeoff. He will instruct you in the TAKEOFF, CLIMB OUT, LEVEL OFF, COURSE CHANGES, DESCENT, APPROACH, and LANDING procedures that make up the bulk of this scenario. Listen to what Professor Calfior has to say about flying techniques. He is trying to help you obtain the best possible score.

FLIGHT PLAN -

This will be a compass and landmark navigation flight. The flight begins with a CROSSWIND departure from runway 8 at Salinas Airport. After departing the pattern, you will fly a course of 360 degrees (due North) and climb to 4500 feet. When the San Luis Reservoir is directly off your right wing, you will turn left to a heading of 300 degrees, and descend to 3500 feet. You will see two mountains in front of you - fly between them. When you emerge from the other side of the mountains, you will need to make an immediate left turn to a heading of 190 degrees (watch the mountain). You will see San Jose International Airport off to your right. When the airport is at your 4 o'clock position, you will turn to the right to enter a 45 for San Jose's runway 12L (Left). You will fly a standard LEFT DOWNWIND pattern with the exception of a shortened BASE leg because of the other runway next to you. After filling out our flight plan in Appendix A, and calling the Flight Service Station (FSS) to file it, we need to turn to Appendix B and locate the sectional map for San Francisco. Find Salinas and San Jose International airports. Read the route of flight carefully and draw the route on the map. After you have finished drawing your route, answer the following questions.

   **   a) What is the name of the airport to your right, about 20 miles into the flight? _____ (15 pts)

   **   b) What is the height of the mountain to your left, as you turn towards San Jose? _____ (15 pts)

   **   c) What is the name of the mountain in question "b"? _____(15 pts)

SETUP

Aircraft:
    1) Choose **"Cessna Skylane RG"**

Weather:
    1) Set Surface winds **"DEPTH"** to **"2000"**
    2) Set Surface winds **"DIR"** to **"040"**
    3) Set Surface winds **"SPEED"** to **"15"**

4) Set Level 1 "**TOPS**" to "**5000**"
5) Set Level 1 "**BASE**" to "**2000**"
6) Set Level 1 "**DIR**" to "**030**"
7) Set Level 1 "**SPEED**" to "**25**"
8) Set Level 2 "**TOPS**" to "**10000**"
9) Set Level 2 "**BASE**" to "**5000**"
10) Set Level 2 "**DIR**" to "**020**"
11) Set Level 2 "**SPEED**" to "**35**"

Aircraft Position:

1) "**NORTH**" to "**16856.0142**" -- [N036° 39' 46.8391]
2) "**EAST**" to "**5159.2588**" -- [W121° 36' 34.3621]
3) "**ALTITUDE**" to "**91**" -- [0]
4) "**HEADING**" to "**260**"

note: At this point you may wish to save this setup for future use.

PREFLIGHT

note: Set **ZOOM** to "**1.0**"
Set **TIME** to "**18:00**"

*"I'm tired after running all the way from Los Angeles - or was I in Chicago? - to out here in San Francisco! Hi! I'm Professor Calfior, and this promises to be an exhilarating, heart pounding, adrenaline flowing visual flight! I've done this flight once before, and there's probably still a deer on that left mountainside, as we turn into San Jose, that is still trying to grow his (or her) hair back where I shaved it close with the left wing!!! Enough flying stories - let's get ATIS on **124.85** and see what's cooking."*

Instruments:

1) Tune **COM** to "**124.85**" (ATIS)

"SALINAS MUNICIPAL, INFORMATION TANGO, 0100 ZULU WEATHER, SKY TWO THOUSAND SCATTERED, VISIBILITY 15. TEMPERATURE 78, WIND 040 AT 15. ALTIMETER 30.10. VASIs ARE OUT OF SERVICE ON RUNWAY 8. ALL AIRCRAFT LANDING AND DEPARTING ON RUNWAY 8. ADVISE ON INITIAL CONTACT YOU HAVE INFORMATION TANGO."

"Did you know that to land on an aircraft carrier, we used VASI type glideslope lights also? They operated by way of a Fresnel lens, you saw amber if you were high, green if you were right on, and red if you were low. Now I've done it, and excited you to Go Navy!! Being a Naval Academy graduate of 1975, it's my lifetime sworn duty to recruit whenever I can!! Well, our VASIs are out, which we wouldn't use for takeoff anyway, so who cares? Let's set up the instruments as we need them, before we taxi to glory!"

2) Set "**Altimeter**" and "**DG**"
3) Set **XPDR** to "**1200**" (VFR code)
4) Tune **NAV 1** to "**117.3**" (SNS)
5) Tune **NAV 2** to "**114.1**" (SJC)
6) Check **CARB HEAT** is "**OFF**" and **GEAR** "**DOWN**"
7) Turn **STROBE** "**ON**" and **LIGHTS** are "**OFF**"

*"Yeah, boy!! We've got just enough daylight to get ourselves over to San Jose, so let's be went! Um, Ground Control frequency is **121.7**, which is fairly generic for most ground controls - 121 point something. Go get us a clearance while I check our route a bit more."*

8) Tune **COM** to "**121.7**" (Salinas Ground)

You:

"SALINAS GROUND, THIS IS CESSNA 13MIKE AT THE TERMINAL, READY TO TAXI TO RUNWAY 8 WITH INFORMATION TANGO."

Salinas Ground:

> **"13MIKE, TAXI TO RUNWAY 8."**

You:

> **"13MIKE."**

TAXI -

"The runway is on your left. You are facing towards the beginning of runway 8. Get some power on, and taxi straight ahead. As you come to the end of the runway, turn left and face the aircraft toward the runway but not on it - in other words, don't cross the hold short line. Then perform your runup."   See Figure 9.1

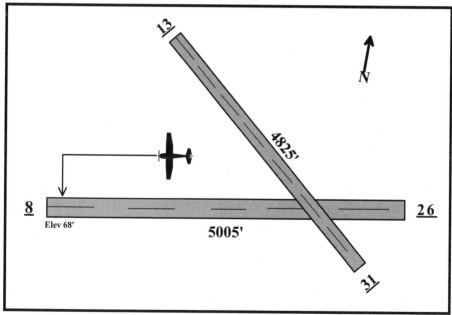

Figure 9.1. Taxi to runway 8

RUN UP -

1) Set brake (hold down to prevent aircraft from moving)
2) Advance power to about "**1750**" RPM
** 3) Select CARB HEAT "**ON**", record RPM drop_____(5 pts)
4) Select CARB HEAT "**OFF**"
** 5) Select "**LEFT**" Mag, record RPM drop_____(5 pts)
6) Select "**BOTH**" Mags
** 7) Select "**RIGHT**" Mag, record RPM drop_____(5 pts)
8) Select "**BOTH**" Mags
9) Reduce power to **idle**
10) Set **FLAPS** to **first notch** (10 degrees takeoff configuration)

"You know, I'm glad you brought that up! No matter how short your flight or how familiar you are with your route, a flight plan should always be filed. If I had hit Bambi on that one flight, and wasn't on a flight plan, then nobody would have known where I was, and consequently not known where to look! Now's a good time to activate our VFR flight plan, don't you think?"

You:

"SALINAS GROUND, 13MIKE WOULD LIKE TO ACTIVATE ITS VFR FLIGHT PLAN TO SAN JOSE INTERNATIONAL AT THIS TIME."

Salinas Ground:

"13MIKE, YOUR VFR FLIGHT PLAN IS NOW ACTIVATED. TIME 0106 ZULU. HAVE A FUN FLIGHT."

*"What a nice guy! Open that vent up there a little more for me, would you? It's kind of hot in here and that air will feel good when we get airborne. Tower frequency is **119.4**, and let's ask for that left crosswind departure, although they probably know that's what we want."*

11) Tune **COM** to "**119.4**" (Salinas Tower)

You:

> "SALINAS TOWER, CESSNA 13MIKE IS READY FOR DEPARTURE RUNWAY 8. WOULD LIKE TO REQUEST A LEFT CROSSWIND DEPARTURE."

Salinas Tower:

> "13MIKE, YOU ARE CLEARED FOR TAKEOFF. MAINTAIN RUNWAY HEADING UNTIL 1100 FEET, THEN LEFT CROSSWIND DEPARTURE APPROVED."

You:

> "13MIKE CLEARED FOR TAKEOFF. STRAIGHT OUT TO 1100 FEET."

FLIGHT

Takeoff:

"Be aggressive with that power and line us up on runway 8. Check your flap settings, we've got full fuel, trimmed for takeoff - so far so good - both oil temperature and oil pressure are in the green. Bye Salinas!"

1) Record TIME _____
2) Release brakes and taxi onto runway 8
3) Advance power to "**FULL**"
4) Maintain centerline of runway
5) At **50 knots** airspeed lift nose wheel off runway
6) At **70 knots** ease back on the yoke to establish a 10 degree pitch up attitude
7) Maintain a climb **AIRSPEED** of **80 knots**
8) Raise **GEAR** when there is no more runway to land on
9) At "**500**" feet above the ground raise the **FLAPS** to "**0**"
10) When "**1000**" feet above the ground, turn **LEFT 90** degrees to depart the traffic pattern

11) When wings are level, reduce power to about **"2300"** RPM

12) Press **"P"** to pause the simulation

** 13) Record your:

ALTITUDE_____(25 pts)

HEADING_____(20 pts)

AIRSPEED_____(15 pts)

VSI_____(15 pts)

FLAPS_____(15 pts)

14) Press **"P"** to continue the simulation

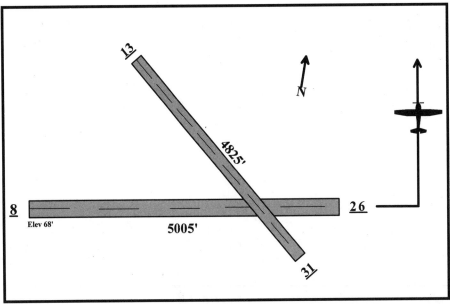

Figure 9.2. Left CROSSWIND departure

"Now, that heading of 360 was, I believe, what you figured out to be the best course out of here to get to that checkpoint of yours abeam the reservoir. So, come right a little bit, and tell me when you see that reservoir. That was very well done all throughout the departure. Oh yeah! Let's see what a 110 knot climb looks like! We'll casually mosey up to altitude!"

Climb out:

1) Increase your airspeed to "**110**" knots
2) Continue your climb to "**4500**" and turn **RIGHT** to a heading of "**360**"

"Remember, always get into the habit of standard rate turns. They may be boring if you're looking for some fun - did I ever tell you about my 130 degree rolls in the gunnery pattern? I'll wait until you're down in the mouth and need some cheering up to tell you!"

Level off:

1) Begin to level off when the altimeter reads "**4400**" feet
2) Maintain "**4500**" feet
3) Reduce power to about "**2200**" **[2400]** RPM

Course:

1) Maintain a heading that will give you a ground track of "**360**"

"On long flights, you may have a tendency to let your mind day dream and lose track of your instruments. Don't let this happen to you, or you may find yourself on the wrong side of a mountain. I happen to be thinking of mountains since I know we're heading toward a couple of them! Keep alert, check signs for what the winds are doing. You may need to make wind corrections. On longish cross countries, the winds can bring to pass large errors in your ground track, and therefore your position."

"Don't fret! You know the reservoir is up ahead somewhere, so just keep working your dead reckoning and pilotage. As long as you're heading north, I would think you certainly can't miss it. Besides, I know exactly where it's at, and so far you're cool!"

2) When the San Luis reservoir is directly off your right wing, start a **LEFT** turn to a heading of "**300**" degrees and descend to "**3500**" feet

"See! And you were worried! There's those two peaks which comes as no surprise, so fly between them very, very, very, very carefully! Notice the emphasis on the word 'ouch' subliminally suggested! In other words, let's not become one with either of those mountains!"

    3) When you emerge from the pass, turn **LEFT** to a heading of "**190**" degrees

"Glory Hallelujah! That was quite a turn, wasn't it? Well again, I knew that and that's why I wanted you to see this! I certainly wouldn't do this with a new kid on the block because it's not exactly the safest way to come into San Jose, but you can't beat the surge of this sort of challenge when you know your limitations. Speaking of San Jose, do you see it out your right window?"

    4) Press "**P**" to pause the simulation

**   5) Record your:

        ALTITUDE_____(25 pts)
        AIRSPEED_____(20 pts)
        VSI_____(20 pts)
        HEADING_____(15 pts)
        RPM_____(15 pts)

6) Press "**P**" to continue the simulation

Descent:

"No need to be at 3500 feet. Drop us down a thousand to 2500 feet. I'm curious to see what ATIS has to say. Oh, I don't know why! I'm just curious!!! No, be careful now! 118.0 is Clearance Delivery. We want 126.95 - focus them eyeballs after our threading the needle trip!"

    1) Descend to "**2500**" feet
    2) Tune **COM** to "**126.95**" (San Jose ATIS)

"SAN JOSE INTERNATIONAL, INFORMATION ROMEO, 0130 ZULU WEATHER, SKY CLEAR, VISIBILITY 20, TEMPERATURE 76, WIND 060 AT 11. ALTIMETER 30.08. ALL LIGHT AIRCRAFT ARE TO LAND ON RUNWAY 12 LEFT, HEAVY AIRCRAFT ON RUNWAY 12 RIGHT. ALL TRAFFIC CONTACT TOWER ON 120.7. ADVISE ON INITIAL CONTACT YOU HAVE INFORMATION ROMEO."

"The real reason why I say it's interesting is because you'll find that landing on runway 12L has a personality all of its own. That's because of runway 12R, which sticks out like a peninsula! And since we're gearing up for a left hand pattern - well, you'll see! Let's check our instruments and call tower before we get inside of their airport traffic area!"

3) Set **ALTIMETER**, set **DG**, and check **FUEL**

"Pretty soon, I'm going to wean you and quit telling you what these frequencies are! Your VFR sectional tells you, Jepps plates tell you, Airport Facility Guides tell you, and in this case ATIS told you. That's why you missed it, because you weren't expecting to hear it on ATIS!! Give your full undivided attention whenever you listen to ATIS! Don't worry, you're doing great! Just a few editorial comments now and then - that's me! Oh yeah, 120.7! After all that, I almost forgot to tell you!"

4) Tune **COM** to "**120.7**" (San Jose Tower)

You:

"SAN JOSE TOWER, THIS IS CESSNA 13MIKE, ABOUT SEVEN MILES NORTHEAST OF THE FIELD AT 2500 FEET, FOR LANDING WITH ROMEO."

San Jose Tower:

"CESSNA 13MIKE, MAKE A 45 DEGREE ENTRY INTO A LEFT DOWNWIND FOR RUNWAY 12 LEFT. DESCEND DOWN TO TRAFFIC PATTERN ALTITUDE WHEN

ESTABLISHED ON THE 45. NEW ALTIMETER SETTING IS 30.06. REPORT WHEN DOWNWIND ABEAM THE TOWER."

You:

"13MIKE, LEFT 45 DEGREE ENTRY FOR RUNWAY 12 LEFT. REMAINING AT 2500 FEET UNTIL ESTABLISHED ON THE 45. WILL REPORT ABEAM THE TOWER."

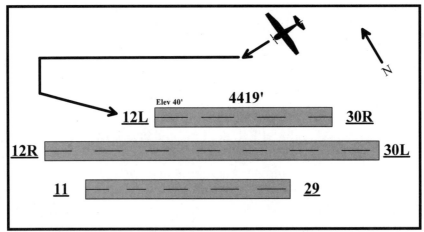

Figure 9.3.   45 degree entry for Left Downwind runway 12I

Approach:

> 5) When the airport is at your 4 o'clock position, turn **RIGHT** and point your airplane at the middle of the airport

"Now isn't this a pretty unique way to get yourself into a landing pattern? That's what I mean about this flight being interesting! I love this route! So, we're on the 45 for a left downwind - let's come down to 1200 feet. Watch the traffic in the pattern - don't trust tower to do all the work for you. Eyes outside."

> 6) Descend to **"1200"** feet
> 7) When the airport fills the screen, turn **RIGHT** to parallel the runway. This will establish your left DOWNWIND leg

"See what I mean about runway 12R? Keep your downwind fairly wide so that you don't inadvertently shortchange yourself on the left base leg. You should be able to see the runway easily out your window. In other words, not hidden under your wing!"

8) Select **GEAR** "**DOWN**" and **CARB HEAT** to "**ON**"
9) Reduce power to about "**1400**" [**1700**] RPM

"Don't forget to call abeam."

You:

"SAN JOSE TOWER, 13MIKE IS ABEAM THE TOWER."

San Jose Tower:

"13MIKE, IN SIGHT, CONTINUE APPROACH. YOUR TRAFFIC IS LEFT DOWNWIND, GETTING READY TO TURN BASE."

You:

"13MIKE HAS TRAFFIC."

10) After slowing to **90 knots,** set **FLAPS** to **first notch**
11) Try and maintain a **400** ft per minute descent

"Adjust your height with power, and your airspeed with pitch. And because of the runways' orientation, it's easy to drift towards the runway right beside us. So concentrate on maintaining that abeam distance until you're ready to turn base."

12) When the end of the runway is at your 7 o'clock position, turn LEFT "**90**" degrees to your **BASE** leg of the approach

** 13) What is your heading for the base leg? _____ (20 pts)
** 14) Will you land with a LEFT or a RIGHT crosswind?
_____ (20 pts)
** 15) Have you been cleared to land yet? _____ (20 pts)

16) Set **FLAPS** to **second notch** (20 degrees)

"ALERT! ALERT! Yikes, Zowee! See runway 12R directly in front of you? I suggest you cautiously make an early LEFT turn to FINAL, sort of dog-leggish! You surely DON'T want to fly into the FINAL approach leg of runway 12R. This could be fatal - besides that, bad!"

17) Press "**P**" to pause the simulation

** 18) Record your:

ALTITUDE_____	(25 pts)
AIRSPEED_____	(20 pts)
VSI_____	(20 pts)
HEADING_____	(25 pts)
CARB HEAT_____	(20 pts)
RPM_____	(20 pts)
FLAPS_____	(15 pts)

19) Press "**P**" to continue the simulation

20) When wings are level, start your LEFT "**90**" degree turn to put you on your **FINAL** leg of the approach

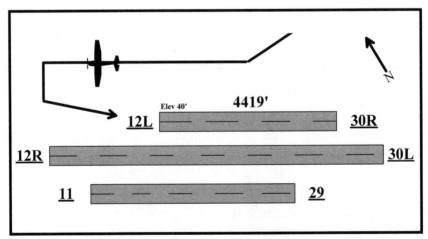

Figure 9.4. Left Downwind turning Left Base for runway 12L

"Yeah, see? You're slightly off to the left side of the runway (which is better than the right side, and probably more healthy!). Don't you worry, even though I'm worried! Joke - get it? Just make any heading corrections to get you lined up with the runway. Remember, stay out of the other runway's air space."

San Jose Tower:

> **"CESSNA 13MIKE, YOU ARE CLEARED FOR LANDING ON RUNWAY 12 LEFT."**

You:

> **"13MIKE, CLEARED TO LAND."**

21) When established on the **FINAL** leg, set **FLAPS** to **third notch** (30 degrees), airspeed should be **70 knots**

"Here comes what I'm known for! SuperGlue your mind to the fact that you always adjust height with power, and airspeed with pitch, while in the landing phase!"

22) When the altimeter displays **"400"** feet, press **"P"** to pause the simulation

** 23) Record your:

AIRSPEED_____(25 pts)
VSI_____(25 pts)
HEADING_____(20 pts)
RPM_____(20 pts)
FLAPS_____(15 pts)
GEAR_____(15 pts)

24) Press **"P"** to continue the simulation

25) When you are 10 to 20 feet off the runway, reduce power to about **"1000"** RPM and start to slowly pitch the nose of the aircraft up to slow your descent and establish a touchdown attitude

"What a nice approach you're flying. I can see you're watching your airspeed real carefully. You don't want to go below what airspeed, ever? That's right - 60 knots! Otherwise, what could happen to you (and me!)? Stall - sink - splat! You got it!"

26) When you are 5 feet off the runway, hold the nose of the aircraft up and allow the airspeed to **SLOWLY** bleed off. Your aircraft will **settle** onto the runway while you follow the centerline

"Let it settle slowly - oh, this is looking good! Little more nose up, establish that landing attitude because we don't want the nose gear to hit first. Oh, looking great!"

27) After touchdown, reduce power to **600 RPM**
28) Apply the brakes and taxi off the active runway to the left
29) Set **CARB HEAT** to "OFF"
30) Set **FLAPS** to "0"

"I'm impressed! You're quite good from what I've seen during this flight! We have another exciting leg to accomplish which will give you some night time experience, and boy, will it ever be pretty! Now switch to Ground Control of 121.7 and get our taxi clearance. While you're at it, close your VFR flight plan with them too."

31) Tune **COM** to "121.7" (San Jose Ground)

You:

"SAN JOSE GROUND, CESSNA 13MIKE IS DOWN AND CLEAR OF RUNWAY 12 LEFT FOR TAXI TO THE TERMINAL. I'D ALSO LIKE TO CLOSE MY VFR FLIGHT PLAN NOW, IF POSSIBLE."

San Jose Ground:

"13MIKE, YOUR VFR FLIGHT PLAN IS CLOSED, AND TAXI TO THE TERMINAL IS APPROVED."

** 32) Record the **TIME**_____(5 pts)

TOTAL POINTS POSSIBLE FOR THIS FLIGHT IS__**575**__

Flight Scenario Ten

San Jose to Oakland

(San Francisco Area - estimated flying time 40 minutes)

Well! Tell Professor Miller how you liked that last flight! Did you make it through the mountains without knocking off any boulders or hit Professor Calfior's deer? And how about that approach into San Jose? Well, get ready for a most interesting <u>NIGHT</u> flight. That's right! Professor Calfior is going to take you on a night flight from San Jose to Oakland via the Golden Gate Bridge. If you are continuing your flight from San Jose, you may skip the section labeled "SETUP" and proceed with Professor Calfior to the section labeled "PREFLIGHT". If this is your first flight of this set, I will lead you through the initial setup phase of the flight simulator where you will set the aircraft type, winds, and position. I will show you how to save this setup, so you may return to the San Jose Airport without going through the initial setup again. Professor Calfior will take you through the PREFLIGHT to set your instruments, TAXI, and perform a RUN UP of the engine prior to takeoff. He will instruct you in the TAKEOFF, CLIMB OUT, LEVEL OFF, COURSE CHANGES, DESCENT, APPROACH, and LANDING procedures that make up the bulk of this scenario. Again I am going to remind you to listen to what Professor Calfior has to say about flying techniques. He is trying to help you obtain the best possible score.

Our route of flight for this scenario takes us over some very interesting night scenery and a LOCALIZER approach into Oakland International Airport.

FLIGHT PLAN -

This will be a night flight utilizing both instrument and landmark navigation skills. The night flight begins with a RIGHT DOWNWIND departure from runway 11 at San Jose International Airport. After departing the pattern, you will fly a course of 260 degrees, while climbing to 4500 feet. Upon reaching the coast line, you will turn right and follow the shore to the Golden Gate Bridge. After flying over the Golden Gate Bridge, Alcatraz, and the Oakland Bay Bridge, you will track inbound on the localizer for runway 11, at Oakland International Airport, to perform a straight in approach. Okay! This sounds good! A night instrument approach to an international airport. GREAT!

Time to get to work. After filling out our flight plan in Appendix A, and calling the Flight Service Station (FSS) to file it, turn to Appendix B and locate the sectional map for San Francisco. Find San Jose International Airport and Oakland International Airport. Carefully draw your route of flight on the map. Check it twice. Now see if you can answer the following questions.

    **   a) What VOR do you fly over before you reach the coast?
                  _____ (15 pts)

    **   b) What is the name of the airport you will fly over on the coast?
                  _____ (15 pts)

    **   c) When you are lined up to land at Oakland, what airport will be to your
          left? _____ (15 pts)

SETUP

Aircraft:
    1) Choose **"Cessna Skylane RG"**

Weather:
    1) Set Surface winds **"DEPTH"** to **"2000"**
    2) Set Surface winds **"DIR"** to **"040"**

3) Set Surface winds "**SPEED**" to "**15**"
4) Set Level 1 "**TOPS**" to "**5000**"
5) Set Level 1 "**BASE**" to "**2000**"
6) Set Level 1 "**DIR**" to "**030**"
7) Set Level 1 "**SPEED**" to "**25**"
8) Set Level 2 "**TOPS**" to "**10000**"
9) Set Level 2 "**BASE**" to "**5000**"
10) Set Level 2 "**DIR**" to "**020**"
11) Set Level 2 "**SPEED**" to "**35**"

10

Aircraft Position:
1) "**NORTH**" to "**17184.5308**" -- [N037° 21' 45.8687]
2) "**EAST**" to "**5164.9918**" -- [W121° 55' 26.8568]
3) "**ALTITUDE**" to "**62**" -- [0]
4) "**HEADING**" to "**300**"

note: At this point you may wish to save this setup for future use

PREFLIGHT

note: Set **ZOOM** to "**1.0**"
Set **TIME** to "**20:45**"

*"It's nighttime - do you know where your airplane is?!! My name is still Professor Calfior, and in an hour and fifteen minutes, it's my bedtime! But this is special, because you and I are going to tour the glittering lights of San Francisco, strafe the Golden Gate Bridge, and patrol the skies overhead to make sure that all inhabitants are safe and sound! Seriously, this will be a great experience for you, and I believe it will strengthen even further your flying skills. Tune in **126.95** in your communications panel and take a listen to ATIS."*

Instruments:

　　1) Tune **COM** to "**126.95**" (ATIS)

"SAN JOSE INTERNATIONAL, INFORMATION VICTOR, 0330 ZULU WEATHER, SKY CLEAR, VISIBILITY 25. TEMPERATURE 71, WIND 040 AT 15. ALTIMETER 30.04. LANDING AND DEPARTING RUNWAY 12 RIGHT. ADVISE ON INITIAL CONTACT YOU HAVE INFORMATION VICTOR."

"Now, what I think would be interesting is to try to get a taxi clearance to runway 11 which is a narrower runway - 100 feet compared to the others' 150 feet. Just to keep it interesting! We'll see if we can - they might say 'No', but it can't hurt to ask, right? By the way, I like your drawing here of going under the Golden Gate Bridge, but we'll probably pass on that mission for tonight! Let's check and set our instruments before we taxi."

　　2) Set "**Altimeter**" and "**DG**"
　　3) Set **XPDR** to "**1200**" (VFR code)
　　4) Tune **NAV 1** to "**113.9**" (OSI)
　　5) Set **NAV 1 OBS** to "**260**" in the upper window
　　6) Tune **NAV 2** to "**113.7**" (PYE)
　　7) Set **NAV 2 OBS to** "**320**" in the upper window
　　8) Set the **DME** to "**NAV 1**" and "**DIST**"
　　9) Check **CARB HEAT** is "**OFF**"
　　10) Check **GEAR** "**DOWN**"
　　11) Turn **STROBE** "**ON**"
　　12) Check **LIGHTS** are "**ON**"

*"Now when we call Ground, since we want to cross the active runway, be prepared to be told to hold short. In other words, you may not be cleared directly nonstop to runway 11. On the other side of the coin, not much is happening out here right now, so if there's nothing to interfere with, then no delays will occur. Just food for thought! Ground Control frequency is the all favorite **121.7**. Whenever you're ready to go. Make sure your little penlight is working - and put in the red cell to conserve your eyes!"*

13) Tune **COM** to "**121.7**" (San Jose Ground)

You:

"SAN JOSE GROUND, THIS IS CESSNA 13MIKE ON THE NORTH SIDE OF RUNWAY 12 LEFT, READY TO TAXI. I'D LIKE TO REQUEST TAXI CLEARANCE TO RUNWAY 11 FOR DEPARTURE. I HAVE INFORMATION VICTOR."

San Jose Ground:

"13MIKE, YOU ARE CLEARED TO RUNWAY 11. PROCEED VIA THE TAXIWAY AND TURN LEFT TO CROSS RUNWAY 12 RIGHT EXPEDITIOUSLY. TOWER FREQUENCY WILL BE 124.0 FOR A RUNWAY 11 DEPARTURE."

You:

"13MIKE, TAXIING."

TAXI -

"Just to verify, runway 12L is to our left, so taxi straight ahead to the end of 12L and turn left so that we cross over the very end of 12L. Continue to taxi straight ahead and cross over runway 12R. Hold short on runway 11. We will perform our runup there. Now as you approach runway 12R, be looking for aircraft on final just in case one has slipped in and we've lost radios, or Ground has missed that problem, or anything else screwy could happen. Never trust anybody fully when being directed around. It'll save your life one day, believe me!!!" See Figure 10.1.

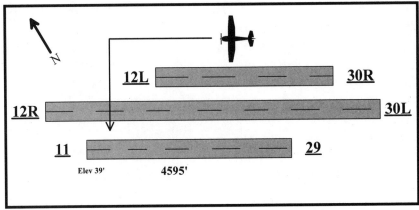

Figure 10.1.   Taxi to runway 11.

RUN UP -

> 1) Set brake (hold down to prevent aircraft from moving)
> 2) Advance power to about **"1750"** RPM
> ** 3) Select CARB HEAT **"ON"**, record RPM drop_____(5 pts)
> 4) Select CARB HEAT **"OFF"**
> ** 5) Select **"LEFT"** Mag, record RPM drop_____(5 pts)
> 6) Select **"BOTH"** Mags
> ** 7) Select **"RIGHT"** Mag, record RPM drop_____(5 pts)
> 8) Select **"BOTH"** Mags
> 9) Reduce power to **idle**
> 10) Set **FLAPS** to **first notch** (10 degrees takeoff configuration)

"Make sure that you turn down the instrument panel lights during night flights. It's all important to be able to conserve your night sight so that you can see rotating beacons and wing lights, and the starship Enterprise while airborne. (Remember Star Trek IV?) Get your flight plan activated with Ground."

You:

"SAN JOSE GROUND, 13MIKE WOULD LIKE TO ACTIVATE ITS VFR FLIGHT PLAN TO OAKLAND INTERNATIONAL."

10

San Jose Ground:

> "13MIKE, YOUR FLIGHT PLAN IS ACTIVATED TO OAKLAND AS OF 2052 LOCAL. HAVE A GREAT FLIGHT."

You:

> "13MIKE, THANK YOU."

> *"So, it's 2052 local. I'll bet you we'll be on the ground at Oakland by a quarter after nine. If I'm wrong, I'll give you a free instruction period. If I'm right, you buy me some gourmet jelly beans! I'm addicted to them! Sound like a deal? Talk to Tower on **124.0**. By the way, did you know that this runway's function is specifically as a touch and go strip?"*

> 11) Tune **COM** to "**124.0**" (San Jose Tower)

You:

> "SAN JOSE TOWER, CESSNA 13MIKE IS AT THE RUNUP FOR RUNWAY 11, READY FOR TAKEOFF."

San Jose Tower:

> "13MIKE, YOU ARE CLEARED FOR TAKEOFF VIA A RIGHT DOWNWIND DEPARTURE. REPORT WHEN PASSING 1100 FEET."

You:

> "13MIKE CLEARED FOR TAKEOFF. WILL REPORT 1100."

FLIGHT

Takeoff:

"Okay, you tell me what we normally check as we start moving out on the centerline of the runway. Yup, flaps are at 10. Well, we haven't got full fuel, so don't use that phrase as a habit, but I'd say about 60 gallons, wouldn't you? Yup, trimmed for takeoff. Upper corner there - that's right! Oil temperature and pressure are in the green, meaning they're normal. Runway sure looks pretty at night with all those blue taxi lights all around! Let's go afterburners!!!!"

1) Record TIME _____
2) Release brakes and taxi onto runway
3) Advance power to "**FULL**" and maintain centerline of runway
4) At **50 knots** airspeed lift nose wheel off runway
5) At **70 knots** ease back on the yoke to establish a 10 degree pitch up attitude
6) Maintain a climb **AIRSPEED** of **80 knots**
7) Raise **GEAR** when there is no more runway to land on
8) At "**500**" feet above the ground raise the **FLAPS** to "**0**"
9) At "**800**" feet above the ground, turn **RIGHT** "**90**" degrees to enter the **RIGHT CROSSWIND** leg of the departure
10) When wings are level, begin your **RIGHT** "**90**" degree turn to the **RIGHT DOWNWIND** leg of the departure

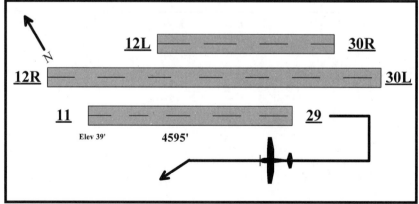

Figure 10.2.   Standard Right Downwind departure.

**   *"You should see the runway out the right window. Remember to tell tower that you're passing through 1100 feet - they just want to make sure you're clear of the pattern altitude. You should be flying parallel to the runway heading, so what heading is that?"* _____ (20 pts)

You:

"SAN JOSE TOWER, 13MIKE IS PASSING 1100 FEET AT THIS TIME."

11) Reduce power to about **"2300"** RPM at **"1000"** feet above the ground (AGL)

12) When you are abeam the midpoint of the runway, turn **LEFT "45"** degrees to depart the pattern. See Figure 10.2.

*"Nice job! Radio calls were sharply stated, you departed on that 45 very cleanly, and good control of that **600** feet per minute climb rate on your Vertical Speed Indicator (VSI). Now organize yourself in the cockpit with your sectional and take us to Oakland!"*

13) Press **"P"** to pause the simulation

**   14) Record your:

NAV 1 DME DIST_____	(25 pts)
ALTITUDE_____	(20 pts)
HEADING_____	(20 pts)
AIRSPEED_____	(15 pts)
VSI_____	(15 pts)
GEAR_____	(10 pts)
FLAPS_____	(10 pts)
MAGS_____	(10 pts)
STROBE_____	(10 pts)
LIGHTS_____	(10 pts)

15) Press **"P"** to continue the simulation

"Good-bye San Jose! Now we know that a course of 260 degrees will bring us to the coastline that we planned for, so go ahead and adjust your 45 degree departure routing now.   At night, you can't use landmarks so readily to tell whether you're drifting or not, so make use of the Number 1 VOR there, and keep the needle centered since '260' is dialed in the window."

Climb out:

1) Turn to a heading of "**260**" degrees, and continue climb to "**4500**" feet

Level off:

1) Begin to level off when the altimeter reads "**4400**" feet
2) Maintain "**4500**" feet
3) Reduce power to about "**2200**" **[2400]** RPM

Course change:

"Watch for the coast line, you'll see its definition with all these stars out. You will be passing the VOR you are tracking, by about five miles, before you reach the coast. So take that into consideration."

1) When you are over the shore line, turn **RIGHT** to parallel the coast ("**320**" degree heading)

"Ah, the gentle, peaceful, scintillating, and cold Pacific! All your turns should be STANDARD RATE. You make this STANDARD RATE turn by keeping the wings on the little airplane displayed on the TURN COORDINATOR aligned with the "R" indicator."

2) When your heading indicator reads "**310**", start to roll out

3) After you have rolled out, press "**P**" to pause the simulation

** 4) Record your:
NAV 1 DME DIST_____(25 pts)
NAV 2 DME DIST_____(25 pts)
ALTITUDE_____(20 pts)
AIRSPEED_____(15 pts)
5) Press "**P**" to continue the simulation

*"Now again, you can use the Number 2 VOR this time - remember, that's why we set it up when we pre-briefed this - to help you maintain the **320** course. You know, if I'm not mistaken, somewhere close by will be the aircraft carrier sort of sitting around! You don't get to see them much in Arizona where I come from - so I'm keen to see it!"*

6) When you are abeam Half Moon Bay Airport, descend to "**3000**" feet

"Yeah, that airport is right on the 39 DME fix from Point Reyes VOR, which is what we have our Number 2 VOR set to. Hey! There's the carrier heading for the Golden Gate Bridge! Fly over that thing! We might fly into some heavy flak, but this is an armored 182 RG! I'm not kidding! Go and fly over it - maybe they'll let us land!"

7) When you are over the aircraft carrier, turn **RIGHT** towards the Golden Gate Bridge
8) Descend to "**2000**" feet
9) Tune your **NAV 1** to "**111.9**" and set **DME** to "**NAV 1**" and "**DIST**"
10) Set the **NAV 1 OBS** to "**114**" in the upper window

*"Fly right over that Golden Gate Bridge! WOW!!! Have you ever seen such a gorgeous sight? It reminds me again of how non-pilots would be sad if they ever really knew what they were missing. Well, we aren't missing it!!! Back to business! Let's get ATIS for Oakland International on **128.5**, and though we'll come in visual for a straight in, I'll show you how this is, in actuality, a localizer approach to runway 11!"*

10

11) Tune **COM** to "**128.5**" (Oakland International ATIS)

"OAKLAND INTERNATIONAL, INFORMATION ECHO, 0415 ZULU WEATHER, SKY CLEAR, VISIBILITY 20, TEMPERATURE 70, WINDS 130 AT 6, ALTIMETER 30.03. RUNWAY 11 IS THE PRIMARY DEPARTURE AND ARRIVAL RUNWAY. ALL ARRIVING VFR TRAFFIC CONTACT TOWER ON 127.2, ALL ARRIVING IFR TRAFFIC CONTACT BAY APPROACH ON 120.9. ADVISE ON INITIAL CONTACT YOU HAVE INFORMATION ECHO."

12) Set **ALTIMETER**, set **DG**, and check **FUEL**
13) Fly over Alcatraz, and turn **RIGHT** to fly over the Oakland Bay Bridge

*"Here's what I'd like you to do. We are VFR, but I'd like to show you, and have you fly a practice localizer approach into Oakland's runway 11! I'll walk you through it. Let's switch to Bay Approach on **120.9** and find out if they'll let us shoot a practice ILS (Instrument Landing System) approach to runway 11 - and they can monitor us for a while. They'll tell us when to go to Tower frequency. So go ahead and give them a call."*

14) Tune **COM** to "**120.9**" (Oakland Bay Approach)

You:

"OAKLAND BAY APPROACH, THIS IS CESSNA 13MIKE, NORTHWEST OF OAKLAND INTERNATIONAL AT 2000 FEET. I'D LIKE TO REQUEST A PRACTICE ILS APPROACH TO RUNWAY 11, OAKLAND INTERNATIONAL WITH A HANDOFF TO TOWER. I AM VFR."

Bay Approach:

"CESSNA 13MIKE, SQUAWK 4451 AND IDENT."

You:

"13MIKE, SQUAWKING 4451 AND IDENTING."

15) Set **XPDR** to **"4451"** (assigned code)

Bay Approach:

"13MIKE, RADAR CONTACT 10 MILES NORTHWEST OF THE FIELD, YOU ARE CLEARED FOR A PRACTICE ILS APPROACH RUNWAY 11 INTO OAKLAND INT'L. REMAIN ON THIS FREQUENCY UNTIL FURTHER NOTICE. STATE YOUR INTENTIONS."

You:

"13MIKE WOULD LIKE TO TERMINATE THIS APPROACH WITH A FULL STOP LANDING. HAVE INFORMATION ECHO."

Bay Approach:

"13MIKE, APPROVED AS REQUESTED. INTERCEPT THE LOCALIZER FROM YOUR PRESENT POSITION AND COMMENCE APPROACH."

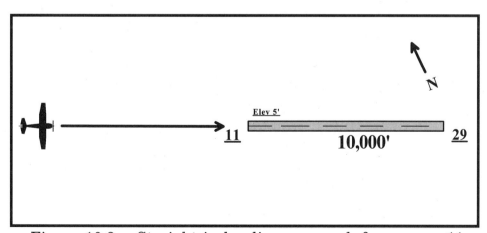

Figure 10.3. Straight in localizer approach for runway 11.

*"Nice job! What's happening now is that we will come in on the localizer course, a heading of **114** degrees, which see - it's straight in to Oakland International! Remember how we set up the Number 1 CDI needle? Being centered tells you that you are flying right down the final approach track. So watch how this looks visually, but I wanted to give you a taste of an instrument approach procedure, even though we are going about it very unorthodoxically! (How do you like that made up word, huh?)*

Approach:

1) When you are over the Oakland Bay Bridge, set **CARB HEAT "ON"** and reduce power to about "**1600**" [**1900**] RPM

2) Maintain a "**500**" feet per minute descent on the VSI

"If you were actually flying the ILS approach as an instrument pilot, the horizontal needle on your Number 1 VOR, should be centered straight across. That tells you that you are on the glideslope of this specific approach. I'm not interested in you taking heed to that. Continue to search for the picture of the approach end of the runway on that special position of your windscreen, and come on down by way of visual cues. But that horizontal glideslope needle won't be far from center if we're on that nice 3 degree glideslope anyway!"

3) When the **NAV 1 DME DIST** reads "**5.0**", reduce power to about "**1400**" [**1700**] RPM

*"Shoot for a "**500**" feet per minute rate of descent on the VSI from this point in. See those traveling lights in front of you? Those are what's called the approach lights for this specific ILS approach, otherwise known as rabbits. Use those to help align yourself to the runway."*

4) Press "**P**" to pause the simulation

** 5) Record your:

AIRSPEED_____(25 pts)
RPM_____(25 pts)
VSI_____(20 pts)
ALTITUDE_____(20 pts)
HEADING_____(15 pts)
CARB HEAT_____(10 pts)
XPDR_____(10 pts)

6) Press "**P**" to continue the simulation

7) When the **NAV 1 DME DIST** reads "**4.0**", select **GEAR "DOWN"**

Bay Approach:

"CESSNA 13MIKE, WE HAVE YOU FOUR MILES FROM THE RUNWAY, SWITCH TO TOWER ON 127.2. SQUAWK 1200. THEY KNOW YOU'RE COMING IN. GOOD NIGHT."

You:

"OAKLAND BAY APPROACH, 13MIKE. THANK YOU FOR ALLOWING US IN. SWITCHING 127.2, SQUAWKING 1200."

8) Tune **COM** to "**127.2**" (Oakland International South Tower)
9) Set **XPDR** to "**1200**" (VFR code)

You:

"OAKLAND TOWER, THIS IS CESSNA 13MIKE ON A FOUR MILE FINAL INBOUND FOR A FULL STOP. I HAVE INFORMATION ECHO."

Oakland Tower:

"CESSNA 13MIKE, HAVE YOU IN SIGHT. YOU ARE CLEARED FOR A FULL STOP RUNWAY 11."

10) When you have slowed to **90** knots set **FLAPS** to **first notch**

*"WOW!! Do you even need me here with you? This is spectacular!!! You're nailed down solidly on that **500** feet per minute rate of descent, and you're very wonderfully adjusting your height with power, and your airspeed with pitch. I should have brought my video camera and taped this for you, just so that you can show it off to your friends! Well, keep it going - man, this is incredible!"*

11) When the **NAV 1 DME DIST** reads "**3.0**", set **FLAPS** to "**20**" degrees

12) When the **NAV 1 DME DIST** reads "**2.0**", set **FLAPS** to "**30**" degrees

13) Press "**P**" to pause the simulation

** 14) Record your:

AIRSPEED_____(25 pts)
RPM_____(25 pts)
VSI_____(20 pts)
ALTITUDE_____(20 pts)
HEADING_____(15 pts)
CARB HEAT_____(10 pts)
GEAR_____(10 pts)

15) Press "**P**" to continue the simulation

"You should be lined up with runway 11, just by following those rabbit lights, but you've got the runway centerline lights and the whole works now! Make slight heading adjustments to compensate for winds, overshoots, or undershoots. And when I say 'slight', I mean real slight!"

16) Airspeed should be **70 knots**

"Oh, so pretty! I don't think I could fly this as nicely as you are! You're an inspiration! Remember - height with power and airspeed with pitch."

17) When the altimeter displays "**200**" feet, press "**P**" to pause the simulation

**   18) Record your:

AIRSPEED_____(25 pts)
VSI_____(25 pts)
HEADING_____(20 pts)
RPM_____(25 pts)
FLAPS_____(15 pts)

19) Press "**P**" to continue the simulation

20) When you are 10 to 20 feet off the runway, reduce power to about "**1000**" RPM and start to slowly pitch the nose of the aircraft up to slow your descent and establish a touchdown attitude

*"Now this airplane has an intense personality! If your airspeed drops below **60** knots, this holographic gloved hand lunges outward from the airspeed indicator and throttles you violently until you correct your airspeed! At night, that can be pretty scary because your first indication will be some unusual pressure on your larynx!!!" Get the point?"*

21) When you are five feet off the runway, hold the nose of the aircraft up and allow the airspeed to **SLOWLY** bleed off. Your aircraft will <u>settle</u> onto the runway while you follow the centerline

"That's it! Be gentle - wear your ballet shoes! Smooth coordination of throttle and nose. Don't be impatient, let the aircraft <u>settle</u> onto the runway slowly."

22) After touchdown, reduce power to **600 RPM**
23) Apply the brakes
24) Turn left and taxi off the active runway
25) When the aircraft has stopped, set **CARB HEAT** to "**OFF**"
26) Set **FLAPS** to "**0**"

10

"What an exciting flight! All I can say is keep up the good work, and I really will consider it a privilege to ever have you as a student for any other flight! You seem to have the big picture, and believe me this will inspire you to also want to continue working with your instruments. Go ahead and switch to Ground on 121.75, get our taxi clearance and close our VFR flight plan."

27) Tune **COM** to "**121.75**" (Oakland International South Ground)

You:

"OAKLAND GROUND, CESSNA 13MIKE IS DOWN AND CLEAR OF RUNWAY 11 FOR TAXI TO THE TERMINAL. PLEASE CLOSE MY VFR FLIGHT PLAN."

Oakland Ground:

"13MIKE, YOUR FLIGHT PLAN IS CLOSED, TAXI TO THE TERMINAL."

** 28) Record the **TIME**_____(5 pts)

TOTAL POINTS POSSIBLE FOR THIS FLIGHT __**675**__

Flight Scenario Eleven

Bridgeport to La Guardia

(New York Area - estimated flying time 55 minutes)

Hey ya! Fa ya New Yok fans, this hyah is Professor Miller, da Brooklyn Boy-o fram dee behst Flaht School! You got to love New York talk! The first flight scenario, of Series Number Four, departs Bridgeport's Sikorsky Memorial Field in Connecticut and arrives at La Guardia Airport in New York City. I will lead you through the initial setup phase of the flight simulator, where you will set the aircraft type, winds, and position. I will show you how to save this setup so you may return to the Bridgeport Airport without going through the initial setup steps. I will then turn you over to Professor Calfior who will take you through the PREFLIGHT of "13MIKE" to set your instruments, TAXI, and perform a RUN UP of the engine prior to takeoff. He will instruct you in the TAKEOFF, CLIMB OUT, LEVEL OFF, COURSE CHANGES, DESCENT, APPROACH, and LANDING procedures that make up the bulk of this scenario. Please listen to what Professor Calfior has to say about flying techniques. He is trying to help you obtain the best possible score.

FLIGHT PLAN -

You are on an IFR flight plan, with weather being excellent. The route of flight follows well established departure, climb, cruise, descent, and landing procedures. The procedures begin with a departure from runway 6 at Bridgeport's Sikorsky Memorial Airport with a right downwind departure, and a climb out to 6000 feet. You will intercept the BRIDGEPORT 212 radial and go outbound until arriving at the KENNEDY 066 radial. Proceed inbound to KENNEDY VOR. While inbound, you will request radar vectors to La Guardia Airport via the RIVER VISUAL RWY 13. You will descend into the various TCAs, in steps to 2,000 feet, and maintain that altitude until acquiring the 312 radial final approach track into La Guardia. After filling out our flight plan in Appendix A, and calling the Flight Service Station (FSS) to file it, we need to turn to Appendix B and locate the sectional map for New York. Find Bridgeport and La Guardia airports. Draw the above route on the map. Now answer these questions.

**   a) What is the name of the body of water you will be crossing from Connecticut to the New York side?_____(15 pts)

**   b) What airspace do you just miss as you turn inbound toward the Kennedy VOR?_____(15 pts)

**   c) What river will you be heading north on to arrive at La Guardia Airport?   _____(15 pts)

SETUP

Aircraft:
1) Choose **"Cessna Skylane RG"**

Weather:
1) Set Surface winds **"DEPTH"** to **"1000"**
2) Set Surface winds **"DIR"** to **"350"**

3) Set Surface winds "**SPEED**" to "**15**"
4) Set Level 1 "**TOPS**" to "**10000**"
5) Set Level 1 "**BASE**" to "**1000**"
6) Set Level 1 "**DIR**" to "**220**"
7) Set Level 1 "**SPEED**" to "**23**"

Aircraft Position:
1) "**NORTH**" to "**17284.9658**" -- [N041° 09' 43.4866]
2) "**EAST**" to "**21248.1564**" -- [W073° 07' 39.7997]
3) "**ALTITUDE**" to "**16**" -- [0]
4) "**HEADING**" to "**240**"

note: At this point you may wish to save this setup for future use.

11

PREFLIGHT

note: Set **ZOOM** to "**1.0**"
Set **TIME** to "**10:00**"

"Can you believe it! I, Professor Calfior, am flying in New York! I was born in this place way back in '53 - 1853!! Of course, most of my friends back then were indians, who were just in negotiation talks about the building of the Empire State Building as a financial real estate investment! Well, enough chatter! Professor Miller is giving me the signal to get on with this before it becomes more than 17 pages, so dial in 119.15 for Bridgeport's Automatic Terminal Information Service - ATIS for short, so we can get some local airport information."

Instruments:

1) Tune **COM** to "**119.15**" (ATIS)

"BRIDGEPORT SIKORSKY MEMORIAL, INFORMATION HOTEL, 1330 ZULU WEATHER, SKY 6000 THIN SCATTERED, VISIBILITY 15. TEMPERATURE 75, WIND 350 AT 15. ALTIMETER 29.86. RUNWAY 11-29 IS CLOSED UNTIL FURTHER NOTICE FOR REPAVING OF SURFACE. LANDING AND DEPARTING RUNWAY 6. ADVISE ON INITIAL CONTACT YOU HAVE INFORMATION HOTEL."

"This gives you about a 70 degree crosswind takeoff in order to get out of here, but at 15 knots, it's not impossible. Maybe by the time we get to the runup of runway 6, the wind will tame down somewhat. But again, if it doesn't - no biggee!! I took off on grass once, so if we slide off the runway, just keep the power on - we'll eventually get airborne! Let's set up the instruments."

2) Set "**Altimeter**" and "**DG**"
3) Tune **NAV 1** to "**108.8**" (BDR)
4) Set **NAV 1 OBS** to "**212**" in the upper window
5) Tune **NAV 2** to "**115.9**" (JFK)
6) Set **NAV 2 OBS** to "**246**" in the lower window
7) Set the **DME** to "**NAV 1**" and "**DIST**"
8) Check **CARB HEAT** is "**OFF**"
9) Check **GEAR** "**DOWN**"
10) Turn **STROBE** "**ON**"
11) Check **LIGHTS** "**OFF**"

"Just for your learning edification, we are filing this flight on an IFR flight plan. We could just as easily be on a VFR flight plan with all this beautiful weather, but you need the experience, in order to not be intimidated by its reputational shadow of doom!!! So when we talk to Ground Control on 121.9 for taxi, also place your IFR clearance on request. That'll give them time to get it, and us time to taxi and get our pretake-off needs met."

12) Tune **COM** to "**121.9**" (Bridgeport Ground)

You:

> "BRIDGEPORT GROUND, CESSNA 13MIKE IS AT THE RAMP, READY TO TAXI TO RUNWAY 6. I'D LIKE TO PLACE MY IFR FLIGHT PLAN ON REQUEST, PLEASE."

Bridgeport Ground:

> "CESSNA 13MIKE, YOU ARE CLEARED TO TAXI TO RUNWAY 6. PROCEED STRAIGHT AHEAD TO THE RUNUP AREA. FLIGHT PLAN ON REQUEST."

You:

> "13MIKE."

TAXI -

> *Runway 6 is to your left. As Ground said, simply proceed along the taxiway to the runup area. Hold short of runway 6 and perform your runup. Just so that you can see the reasoning behind this, it's practical to have filed on an IFR flight plan. Being unfamiliar with the New York area, we will be able to enter all the Terminal Control Areas near Kennedy and La Guardia with IFR control by our ears!! Okay, what do we have to do?"* See Figure 11.1

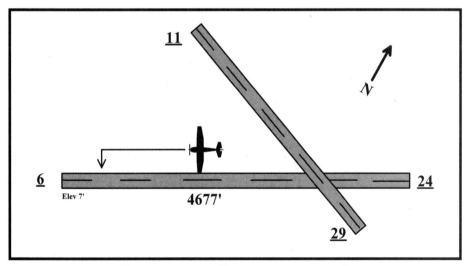

Figure 11.1. Taxi to runway 6.

RUN UP -

1) Set brake (hold down to prevent aircraft from moving)
2) Advance power to about "**1800**" RPM
** 3) Select CARB HEAT "**ON**", record RPM drop_____(5 pts)
4) Select CARB HEAT "**OFF**"
** 5) Select "**LEFT**" Mag, record RPM drop_____(5 pts)
6) Select "**BOTH**" Mags
** 7) Select "**RIGHT**" Mag, record RPM drop_____(5 pts)
8) Select "**BOTH**" Mags
9) Reduce power to **idle**
10) Set **FLAPS** to **first notch** (10 degrees takeoff configuration)

Bridgeport Ground:

**"CESSNA 13MIKE, ADVISE WHEN READY TO COPY YOUR
IFR CLEARANCE."**

*"Talk about timing! That's about as perfect as Ground could get. I'll
back you up on the copying of your clearance, but if you have any
questions or miss something, just ask Ground to repeat whatever
portion you need. But as we've briefed in the restaurant, it's a pretty
standardized briefing format. You better respond before they think
we've died!"*

You:

"BRIDGEPORT GROUND, 13MIKE IS READY TO COPY."

Bridgeport Ground:

**"CESSNA 13MIKE IS CLEARED TO THE LA GUARDIA
AIRPORT AS FILED. UPON TAKEOFF, MAINTAIN
RUNWAY HEADING TO 700 FEET, THEN TURN RIGHT TO
INTERCEPT THE VICTOR 229 AIRWAY TO KENNEDY VOR.
CLIMB UP TO AND MAINTAIN SIX THOUSAND FEET.
DEPARTURE CONTROL FREQUENCY WILL BE 126.95.
SQUAWK 2323."**

You:

> **"CESSNA 13MIKE IS CLEARED TO LA GUARDIA AS FILED. ON TAKEOFF, MAINTAIN RUNWAY HEADING TO 700 FEET, THEN RIGHT TURN FOR VICTOR 229 TO KENNEDY. CLIMB TO AND MAINTAIN SIX THOUSAND FEET. DEPARTURE ON 126.95, SQUAWK 2323."**

Bridgeport Ground:

> **"READ BACK IS CORRECT, 13MIKE.   ENJOY YOUR FLIGHT."**

> *"WOW!! Did you hear yourself?? Well, of course you did! But that was better than I've heard most experienced IFR gents, or ladies handle an IFR read back! I have this feeling you are going to surprise me all throughout this flight. Quite a load of confidence - and believe me, that's what's needed, so don't ever lose that! If you're set, let's go to Tower on 120.9 and start our journey."*

> 11) Set **XPDR** to "**2323**" (assigned code)
> 12) Tune **COM** to "**120.9**" (Bridgeport Tower)

You:

> **"BRIDGEPORT TOWER, CESSNA 13MIKE IS NUMBER ONE FOR RUNWAY 6, READY TO TAKEOFF, RIGHT DOWNWIND DEPARTURE."**

Bridgeport Tower:

> **"13MIKE, TAXI INTO POSITION AND HOLD."**

You:

> **"13MIKE, POSITION AND HOLD."**

> 13) Release brakes and taxi onto runway 6

FLIGHT

Takeoff:

"Rather than running this takeoff on the go, add your power and line us up on the runway centerline, but no full power trip as we round the corner! We can still check our flap settings at 10 degrees, fuel is chock full, trimmed for takeoff, and those two arrows for oil temperature and pressure are faithfully at rest on the green! I'd expect pretty soon now - like on seven! One, two, three, four, five, six ..."

Bridgeport Tower:

"CESSNA 13MIKE, YOU ARE CLEARED FOR TAKEOFF."

You:

"13MIKE IS CLEARED FOR TAKEOFF."

"See!!!!!!!!"

1) Record TIME _____
2) Advance power to **"FULL"**
3) Maintain centerline of runway
4) At **50 knots** airspeed lift nose wheel off runway
5) At **70 knots** ease back on the yoke to establish a 10 degree pitch up attitude
6) Maintain a climb **AIRSPEED** of **80 knots**
7) Raise **Gear** when there is no more runway to land on
8) Check behind you to ensure you've maintained runway centerline
9) At **"500"** feet above the ground raise the **FLAPS** to **"0"**
10) Reduce power to about **"2300"** RPM at **"1000"** feet above the ground (AGL)

"This should give you approximately an "800" feet per minute climb rate on your Vertical Speed Indicator (VSI). Now, Tower will come back to you with a change to Departure Control when they're ready. Meanwhile, just follow your departure clearance given to you, and enjoy the view of the Long Island Sound."

Climb out:

1) Maintain runway heading to "**700**" feet above the ground
2) Then commence a **RIGHT** turn to the CROSSWIND

"All turns should be STANDARD RATE. You make a STANDARD RATE turn by keeping the wings on the little airplane displayed on the TURN COORDINATOR aligned with the "R" indicator. Keep your head on a swivel and look for traffic. We are not in radar control yet - it's only tower who has us, but even then - never rely upon Big Brother on radar to 100% give us the collision avoidance protection of an entire flight!"

3) When wings are level on the crosswind, check for traffic and then turn further **RIGHT** to the DOWNWIND

Bridgeport Tower:

"CESSNA 13MIKE, SWITCH TO NEW YORK DEPARTURE CONTROL FREQUENCY AT THIS TIME."

You:

"13MIKE SWITCHING. GOOD DAY."

4) Tune **COM** to "**126.95**" (New York Departure)

You:

"DEPARTURE CONTROL, CESSNA 13MIKE IS WITH YOU. PASSING 1900 FOR 6000."

New York Departure:

> **"CESSNA 13MIKE, RADAR CONTACT ONE MILE SOUTHEAST OF BRIDGEPORT, REPORT WHEN LEVEL AT 6000 FEET."**

You:

> **"13MIKE."**

**   5) Maintain your DOWNWIND heading _____ (20 pts) until the **NAV 1 CDI** needle **centers**
            6) Track outbound on the "212" radial (same course) that your **NAV 1 OBI** is displaying

"The reason you could wait as you did for the needle to center before turning is because it was only a 30 degree turn. You're not going to overshoot anything at that rate! Anyway, remember that to track inbound on a VOR radial, you keep the CDI needle centered by making minor heading changes to compensate for winds. You know the rules by now, so I won't bore you with my oration!"

Level off:

     1) Begin to level off when the altimeter reads "**5900**" feet
     2) Maintain "**6000**" feet
     3) Reduce power to about "**2200**" **[2400]** RPM

You:

> **"NEW YORK DEPARTURE, CESSNA 13MIKE IS LEVEL AT 6000 FEET."**

New York Departure:

> **"CESSNA 13MIKE, SWITCH TO BOSTON CENTER ON 124.5."**

You:

> **"13MIKE, SWITCHING 124.5"**

4) Tune **COM** to "**124.5**" (Boston Center)

You:

"BOSTON CENTER, CESSNA 13MIKE IS WITH YOU AT 6000 FEET."

Boston Center:

"13MIKE, RADAR CONTACT."

"Does that surprise you? These Centers try to say as little as possible if they can help it, because of the amount of traffic they have to deal with. I mean, listen to all that verbiage you're hearing. One word of caution, you do listen to it with some focus, because in the midst of all that communication, all of a sudden, you'll hear your call sign and you want to get it the first time! That's the law up here in the IFR structure of communication LA-LA land!!"

11

Course change:

**   1) When level at "**6000**", record your Ground speed _____ (20 pts), and heading for a centered CDI needle _____ (20 pts)

2) When the **NAV 2 CDI** needle is centered, commence a turn to a heading of "**246**" and track inbound to **JFK VOR**

3) Set the **DME** to "**NAV 2**"

4) When established inbound, press "**P**" to pause the simulation

**   5) Record your:

        NAV 2 DME DIST_____(25 pts)
        ALTITUDE_____(20 pts)
        AIRSPEED_____(20 pts)
        COM FREQUENCY_____(20 pts)
        XPDR CODE_____(20 pts)

6) Press "**P**" to continue the simulation

Boston Center:

> **"CESSNA 13MIKE, SWITCH TO NEW YORK CENTER ON 119.8 AT THIS TIME."**

You:

> **"13MIKE, SWITCHING 119.8"**

> 7) Tune **COM** to **"119.8"** (New York Center)

"I continue to be impressed with your radio discipline and conciseness. You are right in always reading back the next assigned frequency, so that if you heard it wrong, Center can correct you before you try for a bum frequency and then have to flail back to the previous one to get the correct one!"

You:

> **"NEW YORK CENTER, CESSNA 13MIKE IS WITH YOU AT 6000 FEET."**

New York Center:

> **"CESSNA 13MIKE, SQUAWK 3165 AND IDENT."**

You:

> **"13MIKE, 3165 AND IDENTING."**

> 8) Set **XPDR** to **"3165"** (new assigned code - and normally push a red IDENT button)

New York Center:

> **"CESSNA 13MIKE, RADAR CONTACT 30 MILES NORTHEAST OF KENNEDY. PROCEED ON COURSE."**

You:

> **"13MIKE."**

"The best way to come into La Guardia, as far as a scenic tour goes, is by way of the River Visual Runway 13 approach. The winds aloft report seems to support our guess that runway 13 will be active. But, it'll depend on what Center and Approach control do with us. They will either clear us for the Visual approach or they won't."

New York Center:

"CESSNA 13MIKE, YOU ARE CLEARED FOR THE RIVER VISUAL RUNWAY 13 APPROACH INTO LA GUARDIA. MAINTAIN PRESENT TRACK INBOUND TO KENNEDY VOR. DESCEND TO AND MAINTAIN 4,000'. SQUAWK 4256. REPORT WHEN OVER JFK VOR."

You:

"13MIKE, CLEARED FOR THE RIVER VISUAL RUNWAY 13, LA GUARDIA. LEAVING 6,000 FEET FOR 4,000 FEET. SQUAWK 4256."

Descent:

9) When "**24**" DME from JFK:

10) Set **XPDR** to "**4256**" (new assigned code)

11) Reduce power to about "**2100**" **[2300]** RPM, descend and maintain "**4000**" feet

"Hold a 400 feet per minute rate of descent during this en route descent, because we are in no hurry to get down. Boy, does this ever look good! I can just barely make out the Jones Beach Monument where I spent many, many hours, when I was growing up! Did you know that Fire Island on our left used to have a nudist colony on it? A friend of mine and I used to fly over it, in a Cessna 152, just to see how revealing they really were! We weren't disappointed!!"

12) Tune **NAV 1** to "**113.1**" (LGA)

13) Set **NAV 1 OBS** to "**132**" in the upper window

14) At "**4000**" feet, set power to about "**2200**" **[2400]** RPM

15) Press "**P**" to pause the simulation

** 16) Record your:

NAV 2 DME DIST_____(25 pts)

NAV 1 DME DIST_____(25 pts)

ALTITUDE_____(20 pts)

AIRSPEED_____(15 pts)

VSI_____(15 pts)

HEADING_____(15 pts)

17) Press "**P**" to continue the simulation

"Let's ask New York Center if we can change frequencies for a short time, to get La Guardia's ATIS information. Frequency 125.95"

You:

"NEW YORK CENTER, CESSNA 13MIKE WOULD LIKE TO SWITCH FREQUENCY FOR A MOMENT, WILL REPORT BACK ON."

New York Center:

"13MIKE, APPROVED. REPORT BACK ON."

18) Tune **COM** to "**125.95**" (La Guardia Arrival ATIS)

"LA GUARDIA INTERNATIONAL, INFORMATION LIMA, 1405 ZULU WEATHER, SKY CLEAR, VISIBILITY 10 WITH HAZE. TEMPERATURE 78, WIND 140 AT 6. ALTIMETER 29.88. LANDING AND DEPARTING RUNWAY 13. ALL INBOUND IFR TRAFFIC, REPORT TO TOWER WHEN OVER CENTRAL PARK. ADVISE ON INITIAL CONTACT YOU HAVE INFORMATION LIMA."

19) Tune **COM** to "**119.8**" (New York Center)

You:

> **"NEW YORK CENTER, CESSNA 13MIKE IS BACK WITH YOU."**

New York Center:

> **"13MIKE."**

> 20) Set **ALTIMETER**, set **DG**, and check **FUEL**

"What makes the IFR environment so easy is that for the most part, Center will lead you by the hand, telling you when to change altitudes, change courses, change frequencies, the whole works. And we are on a Visual approach, so we can see everything real clearly!! So enjoy the ride and follow the instructions given to you implicitly. I am astounded how well you are doing on this pseudo instrument clearance style of flight! Good, good job!"

> 21) When your **NAV 2 DME DIST** reads "**1.5**", you will receive the following clearance:

New York Center:

> **"CESSNA 13MIKE, UPON CROSSING JFK VOR, TURN OUTBOUND TO A MAGNETIC COURSE OF 250. MAINTAIN 4,000 FEET. EXPECT FURTHER CLEARANCE IN FIVE MINUTES."**

You:

> **"13MIKE, OUTBOUND COURSE 250 OVER JFK. HOLD 4,000 FEET."**

Approach:

> 1) When the **NAV 2 DME DIST** reads "**0.4**", turn to a course of "**250**"

2) When you are abeam of the New York land mass with the Hudson River going north, and the Statue of Liberty far abeam on your right, the following clearance will be received:

New York Center:

> "CESSNA 13MIKE, TURN RIGHT TO A HEADING OF 315, DESCEND TO 2,000 FEET AND REPORT WHEN THE STATUE IS IN SIGHT."

You:

> "13MIKE, RIGHT TO HEADING OF 315, LEAVING FOUR FOR TWO. STATUE IS IN SIGHT."

3) Reduce power to about "**2000**" [**2200**] RPM and begin a "**500**" FPM rate of descent
4) Set **CARB HEAT** to "**ON**"

New York Center:

> "13MIKE, SWITCH TO NEW YORK APPROACH CONTROL ON 120.8. GOOD DAY."

You:

> "13MIKE SWITCHING 120.8. THANKS FOR YOUR HELP."

5) Tune **COM** to "**120.8**" (New York Approach Control)

You:

> "NEW YORK APPROACH, CESSNA 13MIKE IS WITH YOU, LEAVING 3300 FOR 2000, APPROACHING THE STATUE."

New York Approach:

> "13MIKE, CONTINUE WITH THE RIVER VISUAL APPROACH, RUNWAY 13."

6) Follow the river, stay to the **LEFT** of the Statue of Liberty

New York Approach:

> **"CESSNA 13MIKE, YOU ARE CLEARED FOR LANDING AT LA GUARDIA INTERNATIONAL RUNWAY 13 VIA THE RIVER VISUAL APPROACH. CONTACT TOWER ON 118.7 AT THIS TIME."**

You:

> **"13MIKE, CLEARED TO LAND. SWITCHING TO TOWER, 118.7. THANKS."**

7) Tune **COM** to "118.7" (La Guardia Tower)

You:

> **"LA GUARDIA TOWER, CESSNA 13MIKE IS APPROACHING CENTRAL PARK AT THIS TIME WITH INFORMATION LIMA."**

La Guardia Tower:

> **"CESSNA 13MIKE, VERIFIED CLEARED TO LAND."**

8) Set power to about "**1800**" **[2100]** RPM and select **GEAR** "**DOWN**"
9) Set **DME** to "NAV 1"

Final approach to a landing:

"What in the heck do you even need an instructor for? It has certainly been a vacation for me here in the right seat!! But, do you see what I mean when it comes to radar vector assistance? It becomes really so much easier, because Air Traffic Control (ATC) has the responsibility of bringing you in. You just fly as tasked, and that's the fun of it all! Now you'll have to transition back to your own decisions. Like watch that Number 1 needle, since we've got it set for the final approach inbound to La Guardia, but you can also see the runway plain as day!"

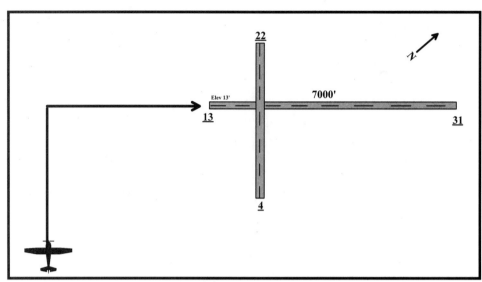

Figure 11.2. RIVER VISUAL APPROACH for runway 13.

10) When the **NAV 1 CDI** needle is three dots **LEFT** of center, turn **RIGHT** to intercept the "**312**" radial, inbound

11) With the field in front of you, correct to the right to line up on runway 13, reduce power to about "**1400**" **[1700]** RPM

12) Begin descent from "**2000**" feet for a straight in landing

13) When you have slowed to **90 knots,** set **FLAPS** to **first notch** (10 degrees)

14) Try and maintain a **600 to 800** ft per minute descent

15) When the **DME** reads "**4.5**" press "**P**" to pause the simulation

** 16) Record your:

AIRSPEED_____	(25 pts)
VSI_____	(25 pts)
ALTITUDE_____	(20 pts)
HEADING_____	(15 pts)
CARB HEAT_____	(15 pts)
RPM_____	(15 pts)
GEAR_____	(15 pts)

17) Press "**P**" to continue the simulation

18) Set **FLAPS** to **second notch** (20 degrees)

"I've got to say it! Watch your descent. Try and maintain the same runway aspect as you continue your descent. Don't let the runway rise or fall. Now you could be a little high, so pull some of that power off and increase your rate of descent, if you have to! That 400 feet per minute is strictly for stabilized on track approaches. Don't hold onto a procedural thought when all evidence is telling you to compensate otherwise!"

19) When passing **400 feet** on the altimeter, set **FLAPS** to **third notch** (30 degrees)
20) Airspeed should be **80** knots

21) Press "**P**" to pause the simulation

** 22) Record your:
AIRSPEED_____(25 pts)
VSI_____(25 pts)
23) Press "**P**" to continue the simulation

"That's it! Adjust height with power, and airspeed with pitch. Wake me up when we land!"

24) When you are 10 to 20 feet off the runway, reduce power to about "**1000**" RPM, and start to slowly pitch the nose of the aircraft up to slow your descent and establish a touchdown attitude

*"I'm awake, being sensitive to the airplane's movements. WATCH YOUR **AIRSPEED**! Be careful not to stall the aircraft. Don't let your airspeed drop below **60 knots**. You'll feel it when it gets below that, because of the mushiness of the airplane - it flies kind of unsettled and feels like it's getting ready to sneeze! We don't want that to happen because what happens to your head when you sneeze? It pulls forward! When this airplane sneezes, its nose also goes down and that's a YIKES!"*

25) When you are five feet off the runway, hold the nose of the aircraft up and allow the airspeed to **SLOWLY** bleed off. Your aircraft will settle onto the runway while you follow the centerline.

*"Nice job on not being impatient and letting the aircraft **settle** onto the runway slowly! That was a nice straight in approach you did. Nice flight altogether!"*

26) After touchdown, reduce power to **600 RPM**
27) Apply brakes, turn right and taxi off the active runway
28) When aircraft has stopped, set **CARB HEAT** to **"OFF"**
29) Set **FLAPS** to **"0"**

*"Now guess what? You don't have to do a blessed thing about closing your IFR flight plan, because the instant you land at an airport that has a control tower, it's automatically closed! I mean to tell you, everything about the instrument environment becomes easy once you understand its techniques and procedures. You have been marvelous this leg! New York must inspire you or something! Flip to Ground Control on **121.7** for taxi instructions."*

30) Tune **COM** to **"121.7"** (La Guardia Ground)

You:

"LA GUARDIA GROUND, CESSNA 13MIKE IS DOWN AND CLEAR OF RUNWAY 13 FOR TAXI TO THE EXECUTIVE AIR TERMINAL."

La Guardia Ground:

"13MIKE, CLEARED TO TAXI TO EXEC AIR TERMINAL."

** 　　31) Record the **TIME**_____(5 pts)

TOTAL POINTS POSSIBLE FOR THIS FLIGHT **525**

Flight Scenario Twelve

La Guardia to Kennedy International

(New York Area - estimated flying time 55 minutes)

Man, oh man! I'm going to miss you all until I see you in the second companion book! For the last time, for this series of flights, I am Professor Miller. This is the second flight scenario of Series Number Four, which departs La Guardia Airport in New York and arrives at JFK International. It's purpose is to give you a fuller taste of the IFR flying environment which is handled exclusively in the IFR flight scenario companion book. If you are continuing on with Professor Calfior, you may skip the SETUP section and proceed to PREFLIGHT. If this is your first flight with "13MIKE", let me tell you how we do the setup. I will lead you through the initial setup phase of the flight simulator where you will set the aircraft type, winds, and position. I will show you how to save this setup so you may return to La Guardia Airport without going through the initial setup steps. I will then turn you over to Professor Calfior who will take you through the PREFLIGHT of "13MIKE" to set your instruments, TAXI, and perform a RUN UP of the engine prior to takeoff. He will instruct you in the TAKEOFF, CLIMB OUT, LEVEL OFF, COURSE CHANGES, DESCENT, APPROACH, and LANDING procedures that make up the bulk of this scenario. Please listen to what Professor Calfior has to say about flying techniques. He is trying to help you obtain the best possible score.

FLIGHT PLAN -

You are on an IFR flight plan in instrument meteorological conditions, and it is nighttime. The route of flight follows well established departure, climb, cruise, descent, and landing procedures. The procedures begin with a departure from runway 13 at La Guardia Airport via the La Guardia Three Departure - (Whitestone Climb) and you will climb and maintain 5,000 feet. Maintain the last heading in the departure clearance until radar vectors are given, which will bring you to the 056 radial of La Guardia VOR. Maintain this track until intercepting the 170 radial out of Carmel VOR, and go back southward over the Long Island Sound. At 25 DME, you will be vectored for a right turn to a heading of 210, in order to fly direct to BABYLON NDB. A descent to 2,500' will be accomplished. Additional vectors will be given via a 315 magnetic course, followed by a clearance to commence the final approach of the instrument approach procedure for VOR DME RWY 22L into JFK International, upon intercepting the 042 radial out of Kennedy. After filling out our flight plan in Appendix A, and calling the Flight Service Station (FSS) to file it, we need to turn to Appendix B, and locate the sectional map for New York. Find La Guardia and Kennedy airports. Draw the above route on the map. Now answer these questions.

**   a) What airport is just on the other side of the New York/Connecticut border by Carmel VOR?_____(15 pts)

**   b) What are the ATIS frequencies for Kennedy?_____(15 pts)

**   c) What is the name of the NDB that is at the departure end of runway 22 at Kennedy?_____(15 pts)

SETUP

Aircraft:

1) Choose **"Cessna Skylane RG"**

Weather:
1) Set Surface winds "**DEPTH**" to "**800**"
2) Set Surface winds "**DIR**" to "**140**"
3) Set Surface winds "**SPEED**" to "**11**"
4) Set Level 1 "**TOPS**" to "**9000**"
5) Set Level 1 "**BASE**" to "**800**"
6) Set Level 1 "**DIR**" to "**080**"
7) Set Level 1 "**SPEED**" to "**25**"
8) Go to "**CLOUDS**"
9) Set Bottom Level - **TOPS** to "**6000**"
10) Set Bottom Level - **BASE** to "**530**"
11) Set Bottom Level - **COVER** to "**overcast**"

Aircraft Position:
1) "**NORTH**" to "**17090.1967**" -- [N040° 46' 43.2995]
2) "**EAST**" to "**21027.4344**" -- [W073° 52' 20.7218]
3) "**ALTITUDE**" to "**29**" -- [0]
4) "**HEADING**" to "**220**"

note: At this point you may wish to save this setup for future use.

PREFLIGHT

note: Set **ZOOM** to "**1.0**"
Set **TIME** to "**19:00**"

"I'm back! Are you ready for a Professor Calfior trivia question? What was the name of JFK International originally? _____ (20 pts). One more! What was the name of the stadium where the New York Mets used to play? _____ (20 pts) Well, this is it! It looks gooey outside, so we will be in the clouds throughout most of this flight. But nighttime is sort of an instrument intensive kind of flight anyway, even if you can see the pretty lights on the ground. So this will continue to expand your wings, so to speak, in a pilot skill form and fashion. Ready for ATIS? It's on 127.05 for all departures, and that's what we be!"

12

Instruments:

1) Tune **COM** to "**127.05**" (ATIS)

"LA GUARDIA INTERNATIONAL, INFORMATION WHISKEY, 2300 ZULU WEATHER, SKY 500 BROKEN, 1000 OVERCAST, RAIN IN ALL QUADRANTS. VISIBILITY TWO MILES, TEMPERATURE 67, WIND 140 AT 11. ALTIMETER 29.82. RUNWAY 13 IS THE ACTIVE RUNWAY FOR ALL DEPARTURES. ADVISE ON INITIAL CONTACT YOU HAVE INFORMATION WHISKEY."

"Maybe we'll be able to pop out of the top of this thing - maybe not! No thunderstorms are present, so we'll be safe, unless you go below 60 knots on final! This is going to be the grand slam flight of all your flights so far! Work on setting up your instruments before we put our IFR clearance on request, and taxi to the runup."

2) Set "**Altimeter**" and "**DG**"
3) Tune **NAV 1** to "**113.1**" (LGA)
4) Set **NAV 1 OBS** to "**056**" in the upper window
5) Tune **NAV 2** to "**116.6**" (CMK)
6) Set **NAV 2 OBS** to "**170**" in the upper window
7) Set the **DME** to "**NAV 1**" and "**DIST**"
8) Check **CARB HEAT** is "**OFF**" and **GEAR** "**DOWN**"
9) Turn **STROBE** "**ON**" and **LIGHTS** "**ON**"

"The red light on our left wing and the green light on our right wing helps other traffic in the air and on the ground to know what our orientation is. Another thing you'll notice is that this airplane will sound a whole bunch quieter in the night when flying. There's just something I can't explain about it, but it's real peaceful and quiet. I think a large percentage of molecules in the air go to sleep at night, so they can't screech as we tickle them going by!"

10) Tune **COM** to "**121.7**" (La Guardia Ground)

You:

> **"LA GUARDIA GROUND, CESSNA 13MIKE IS AT THE RAMP, READY TO TAXI WITH INFORMATION WHISKEY. I'D LIKE TO PLACE MY IFR CLEARANCE ON REQUEST."**

La Guardia Ground:

> **"CESSNA 13MIKE, TAXI TO RUNWAY 13. HOLD SHORT OF RUNWAY 4. YOUR CLEARANCE IS ON REQUEST."**

You:

> **"13MIKE, WILL HOLD SHORT OF RUNWAY 4."**

TAXI -

> *"Runway 13 is to your back. Make a right turn and taxi to the runup area of runway 13. Remember, don't go crossing runway 4 until Ground clears us across. Another thing I love about the nighttime is the blue taxiway lights. Gives an airport a certain pizzazz!"*
> See Figure 12.1

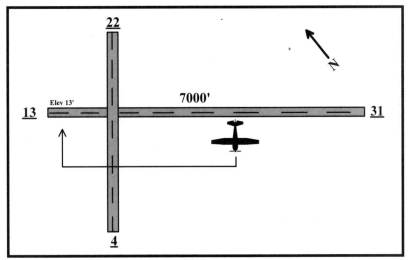

Figure 12.1. Taxi to runway 13.

La Guardia Ground:

> **"CESSNA 13MIKE, CROSS RUNWAY 4 FOR 13. ADVISE WHEN READY TO COPY CLEARANCE."**

You:

> **"13MIKE, CLEARED TO CROSS."**

"Let's go through the runup first, and then once the airplane is taken care of, we have plenty of time to get our IFR clearance before going for it! Sound good? Well, it is!"

RUN UP -

1) Set brake (hold down to prevent aircraft from moving)
2) Advance power to about **"1700"** RPM
** 3) Select CARB HEAT **"ON"**, record RPM drop_____(5 pts)
4) Select CARB HEAT **"OFF"**
** 5) Select **"LEFT"** Mag, record RPM drop_____(5 pts)
6) Select **"BOTH"** Mags
** 7) Select **"RIGHT"** Mag, record RPM drop_____(5 pts)
8) Select **"BOTH"** Mags and reduce power to **idle**
9) Set **FLAPS** to **first notch** (10 degrees takeoff configuration)

"Get your piece of paper ready to copy down your clearance. It's always good to build that habit, because sometimes they come back with some of the most disconcerting changes possible! So work on getting it fully on the first reading, and you'll end up impressing yourself as well as everybody else within range!"

You:

> **"LA GUARDIA GROUND, CESSNA 13MIKE IS READY TO COPY CLEARANCE."**

La Guardia Ground:

> **"CESSNA 13MIKE IS CLEARED TO THE KENNEDY INTERNATIONAL AIRPORT VIA THE LA GUARDIA THREE DEPARTURE - WHITESTONE CLIMB. EXPECT RADAR**

VECTORS IN ACCORDANCE TO YOUR FILED TRAINING ROUTE AFTER YOUR DEPARTURE. DEPARTURE CONTROL FREQUENCY IS 120.4. SQUAWK 5316."

You:

"LA GUARDIA GROUND, CESSNA 13MIKE IS CLEARED TO KENNEDY, WHITESTONE CLIMB, LA GUARDIA THREE DEPARTURE. RADAR VECTORS AFTER DEPARTURE. 120.4 DEPARTURE CONTROL - SQUAWK 5316."

La Guardia Ground:

"13MIKE, READ BACK IS CORRECT. SWITCH TO TOWER AT YOUR CONVENIENCE FOR TAKEOFF CLEARANCE."

> 10) Set **XPDR** to "**5316**" (IFR code)

> 11) Tune **COM** to "**118.7**" (La Guardia Tower)

"Good going! Now this is a training flight, as you're well aware of. Normally, we go pretty direct to Kennedy without messing around flying towards Carmel VOR and Babylon NDB, but it's a round robin style of exercise which ATC is always more than willing to accommodate! So we will be doing this by the seat of our pants as we go, and we can change anything we want to as long as it doesn't conflict with the existing traffic's safety concerns. I'm ready to go! If you are, then we are ready to go, and let's let Tower in on our secret that we're ready to go!!!"

You:

"LA GUARDIA TOWER, CESSNA 13MIKE IS HOLDING SHORT OF RUNWAY 13, READY FOR TAKEOFF, IFR CLEARANCE."

La Guardia Tower:

"CESSNA 13MIKE, YOU ARE CLEARED FOR TAKEOFF. IMMEDIATE RIGHT TURN APPROVED AS PER LA GUARDIA THREE DEPARTURE OR AT PILOT'S DISCRETION. CONTACT DEPARTURE CONTROL WHEN ADVISED."

12

You:

"13MIKE IS CLEARED FOR TAKEOFF. THANKS."

FLIGHT

Takeoff:

"Don't leave any skid marks on the way out to the runway, but you can start putting in the power, and we'll roll as we go. In the process of that move, check that your flap settings are correct - I see they're a notch down, fuel is okay for this flight to Kennedy, trimmed the way you like it, and those wonderful oil temperature and pressure needles love that green spot!"

1) Record TIME _____
2) Release brakes and taxi onto runway 13
3) Advance power to **"FULL"**
4) Maintain centerline of runway
5) At **50 knots** airspeed lift nose wheel off runway
6) At **70 knots** ease back on the yoke to establish a 10 degree pitch up attitude
7) Maintain a climb **AIRSPEED** of **80 knots**
8) Do a climbing **RIGHT** turn to a heading of "175" degrees
9) Raise **Gear** when there is no more runway to land on
10) At "500" feet above the ground, raise the **FLAPS** to "0"

La Guardia Tower:

"CESSNA 13MIKE, SWITCH TO DEPARTURE CONTROL FREQUENCY AT THIS TIME. HAVE A GOOD NIGHT."

You:

"SWITCHING"

11) Tune **COM** to **"120.4"** (New York Departure)
12) Reduce power to about **"2300"** RPM at **"1000"** feet above the ground (AGL)

You:

> **"NEW YORK DEPARTURE, CESSNA 13MIKE IS WITH YOU, PASSING 800 FEET, WHITESTONE CLIMB."**

New York Departure:

> **"CESSNA 13MIKE, RADAR CONTACT. CONTINUE WITH STANDARD INSTRUMENT DEPARTURE."**

You:

> **"13MIKE."**

"Maybe you haven't noticed, but this "800" feet per minute climb rate on your Vertical Speed Indicator (VSI) is always what the needle goes for at this 80 knot climb! An airplane can be so predictable, once you've flown it often enough. It sort of becomes an extension of you, if you know what I mean! That's the factor of comfortableness setting in, which is the mark of a great pilot. Okay, just keep following the instructions of the La Guardia Three Departure as I give them to you."

Climb out:

> 1) Maintain a heading of "**175**" until passing "**1500**" feet, or **NAV 1 DME DIST** reads "**3.0**", whichever comes first
> 2) Then commence a left turn to a heading of "**040**"

"Now here's what's a little bit different from your previous flights! See how really dark it is as we enter the clouds? No visual horizon reference. So you have to fly your attitude indicator, keeping wings level, or when turning, just lock in on your first index mark on the turn coordinator for that standard rate turn. Something else, you can turn "OFF" your STROBES while flying in heavy overcast, in order to prevent the distraction of the resultant flashes. You are looking great, relying upon those instruments - I see more of a crease on your forehead than before, as you concentrate on those instrument readings!"

New York Departure:

> **"CESSNA 13MIKE, HAVE YOU THREE MILES SOUTHEAST OF LA GUARDIA, SWITCH TO NEW YORK CENTER ON 119.8."**

You:

> **"13MIKE, SWITCHING CENTER ON 119.8."**

> 3) Tune **COM** to **"119.8"** (New York Center)

You:

> **"NEW YORK CENTER, CESSNA 13MIKE IS WITH YOU, PASSING 2,500 FEET."**

New York Center:

> **"CESSNA 13MIKE, RADAR CONTACT. CONTINUE ON PRESENT COURSE UNTIL INTERCEPTING THE 056 RADIAL, LA GUARDIA VOR, AND PROCEED OUTBOUND TO INTERCEPT THE 170 RADIAL OUTBOUND FROM CARMEL VOR. CLIMB TO AND MAINTAIN 5,000 FEET. REPORT WHEN LEVEL AT 5,000 FEET."**

You:

> **"13MIKE, INTERCEPT THE LA GUARDIA 056 RADIAL, THEN CARMEL 170 RADIAL OUTBOUND. PASSING 2,900 FEET FOR 5,000 FEET."**

> 4) Watch your **NAV 1 CDI**, when the needle is centered, start your **RIGHT** turn to a heading of **"056"**

> 5) Track outbound on the **"056"** radial

"Flying instruments reminds me of one of those automatic teller machines! You know, you put your card in, punch in some keys, and the money you want comes out to you. We file an IFR flight plan, it's verified by Center, and now they spit out the instructions which we have placed in our flight plan. All we do is obey and trust their instructions - but check your money!!! Looks like we're coming up on our altitude - don't roller coaster over the top on me!"

Level off:

1) Begin to level off when the altimeter reads "**4900**" feet
2) Maintain "**5000**" feet
3) Reduce power to about "**2200**" [**2400**] RPM

You:

"NEW YORK CENTER, CESSNA 13MIKE IS LEVEL AT 5,000 FEET."

New York Center:

"13MIKE, ROGER."

Course changes:

1) When the **NAV 2 CDI** needle is **one and a half** dots **LEFT** of center, turn to "**170**" and track outbound from **CMK VOR**
2) Set the **DME** to "**NAV 2**"
3) When established outbound, press "**P**" to pause the simulation
** 4) Record your:
GROUND SPEED_____(25 pts)
NAV 2 DME DIST_____(25 pts)
ALTITUDE_____(20 pts)
AIRSPEED_____(20 pts)
CURRENT HEADING_____(20 pts)
COM FREQUENCY_____(20 pts)
RPM_____(15 pts)
5) Press "**P**" to continue the simulation

New York Center:

> **"CESSNA 13MIKE, UPON REACHING 25 DME FROM CARMEL, DESCEND DOWN TO AND MAINTAIN 2,500 FEET, AND TURN TO A HEADING OF 210. YOU ARE CLEARED TO THE BABYLON NDB. EXPECT FURTHER CLEARANCE FOR VOR DME RWY 22L APPROACH IN FIFTEEN MINUTES."**

You:

> **"13MIKE, WHEN AT CARMEL 25 DME, DESCEND TO 2,500 FEET, AND TURN TO 210 FOR BABYLON NDB. FURTHER CLEARANCE IN 15 MINUTES."**

"You know what's happened here? Normally, Center will wait until you're closer to get a clearance such as that. But it is on our flight plan, and so they're just saving time for themselves by communicating now. You just need to hold that thought until you reach 25 DME before leaving 5,000 feet altitude. It's still pretty dark out here - and I think it'll probably continue to be dark until morning!!!

Descent:

1) When **NAV 2 DME DIST** reads "25.0", turn **RIGHT** to a heading of "**210**"
2) Set **ADF** to "**275**"
3) Press "**P**" to pause simulation
4) Activate "**ADF**"
5) Press "**P**" to resume simulation
6) Set power to about "**2100**" **[2300]** RPM, descend to "**2500**" ft

"There's a bit of a rush in this descent, so just pick a 1000 feet per minute rate of descent and stabilize yourself."

7) Turn to a heading that will put the arrow of the **ADF** needle straight up on "**0**"

"This is called 'homing'. When homing, many times the course may periodically change due to winds. But it's also an easy method because you're not trying to set a crab to hold a certain radial. You let the winds blow you hither, thither, and yonder, but just keep the ADF needle pointed straight up! You know, if you have tools to use in your aircraft, use them all, or at least know how to use them!"

8) Maintain a centered **ADF** needle

"If the ADF needle is right of straight up, correct your heading to the right. If it's left of straight up, correct to the left. Correct in the direction the needle actually is. Doesn't this give you a warm, fuzzy feeling on the inside?"

9) When passing "**3500**" feet, press "**P**" to pause the simulation

** 10) Record your:

NAV 2 DME DIST_____	(25 pts)
ADF Needle Position_____	(25 pts)
AIRSPEED_____	(20 pts)
VSI_____	(20 pts)
RPM _____	(20 pts)
HEADING_____	(15 pts)

11) Press "**P**" to continue the simulation

12) Tune **NAV 1** to "**115.9**"
13) Set **NAV 1 OBS** to "**232**"
14) At "**2500**" feet, increase power to about "**2200**" [**2400**] RPM

New York Center:

"CESSNA 13MIKE, UPON CROSSING BABYLON NDB, TURN TO A MAGNETIC COURSE OF 315. THIS WILL BE A VECTORED INTERCEPT FOR A FINAL APPROACH INBOUND TO KENNEDY'S VOR DME RWY 22L APPROACH. MAINTAIN 2,500 FEET."

12

You:

> "CESSNA 13MIKE, FROM BABYLON, TURN TO 315 COURSE FOR INTERCEPT TO KENNEDY VOR DME APPROACH, RUNWAY 22 LEFT. MAINTAIN 2,500 FEET. REQUEST PERMISSION TO SWITCH FREQUENCIES FOR A MINUTE. WILL REPORT BACK ON."

New York Center:

> "13MIKE, FREQUENCY CHANGE IS APPROVED. REPORT BACK ON."

> 15) Tune **COM** to "**128.7**" (Kennedy ATIS)

> "KENNEDY INTERNATIONAL, INFORMATION OSCAR, 2320 ZULU WEATHER, SKY 600 OVERCAST, 2000 OVERCAST, LIGHT DRIZZLE, VISIBILITY A MILE AND A HALF. TEMPERATURE 64, WIND 200 AT 10. ALTIMETER 29.81. LANDING AND DEPARTING RUNWAY 22 RIGHT. ALL INSTRUMENT APPROACHES FOR LIGHT AIRPLANES WILL BE ON RUNWAY 22 LEFT. ADVISE ON INITIAL CONTACT YOU HAVE INFORMATION OSCAR."

> *"So you see, that's why Center told us we'd be set up for runway 22 Left! Because there are approaches into 22 Right, whose runway is longer, but we don't need all that length. Plus it keeps us out of harm's way (Do you remember John Wayne - 'In Harm's Way'?) from the monster carriers who tend to eat up little 182 RGs trying to mind their own business! I know that Center is in tears over having lost us, so let's help them dry those tear with joyous news of our return!"*

> 16) Tune **COM** back to "**119.8**"

You:

> "NEW YORK CENTER, CESSNA 13MIKE IS BACK WITH YOU."

New York Center:

"13MIKE, THANK YOU."

> 17) Set **ALTIMETER**, set **DG**, and check **FUEL**
> 18) Set **CARB HEAT** to **"ON"**
> 19) Watch the **ADF** needle. When it falls left or right **"90"** degrees - turn **RIGHT** to a heading of **"315"**
> 20) Set **DME** to **"NAV 1"**

Approach:

New York Center:

> **"CESSNA 13MIKE, UPON INTERCEPTING THE 042 RADIAL OUT OF KENNEDY, YOU ARE CLEARED FOR THE VOR DME RWY 22 LEFT APPROACH INTO JFK INTERNATIONAL. CONTACT NEW YORK APPROACH CONTROL ON 127.4."**

You:

> **"13MIKE, WITH THE 042 JFK RADIAL, CLEARED FOR THE VOR DME RUNWAY 22 LEFT APPROACH. 127.4 NEW YORK APPROACH CONTROL."**

> 1) Tune **COM** to **"127.4"** (New York Approach Control)

You:

> **"NEW YORK APPROACH, CESSNA 13MIKE IS NORTHWEST OF THE FIELD INBOUND FOR THE VOR DME RUNWAY 22 LEFT INTO JFK."**

New York Approach:

> **"CESSNA 13MIKE, VERIFIED 10 MILES NORTHWEST OF THE FIELD, CONTINUE."**

"Great! The approach is ours! I'll walk you through the steps, so just follow my instructions as if I was the page that had the instrument approach procedure on it! You'll like this!"

2) When the **NAV 1 CDI** needle is **two** dots to the **RIGHT**, turn to a heading of "**232**"

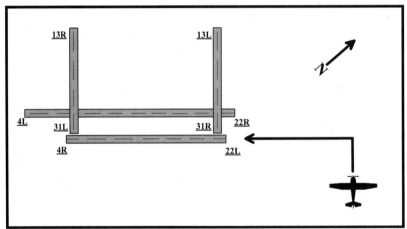

Figure 12.2   VOR DME RWY 22L approach

*"Wahoo! Mountain Dew! You are now on the VOR DME approach. I'd suggest that you now turn your **STROBES** back to the "ON" position so that you're visible and legal!!!"*

3) Reduce power to about "**1500**" **[1800]** RPM and descend to "**2000**" feet

note: You need to be at 2000 feet by the time your **NAV 1 DME DIST** reads "**7.0**" (This is **WUGAL** intersection)

4) When at "**7.0**" DME, put **GEAR** "**DOWN**"
5) When you have slowed to **90 knots,** set **FLAPS** to **first notch**
6) At "**7.0**" DME, continue descent to "**1400**" feet
7) You should be at "**1400**" feet when the **NAV 1 DME DIST** reads "**5.0**" (This is **RUSHY** intersection)

New York Approach:

> **"CESSNA 13MIKE, SWITCH TO TOWER AT THIS TIME ON FREQUENCY 119.1"**

You:

> **"13MIKE, 119.1 TOWER."**

> 8) Tune **COM** to "119.1" (Kennedy Tower)

You:

> **"KENNEDY TOWER, CESSNA 13MIKE IS WITH YOU."**

Kennedy Tower:

> **"CESSNA 13MIKE, YOU ARE CLEARED TO LAND ON RUNWAY 22 LEFT."**

You:

> **"13MIKE, CLEARED TO LAND."**

> 9) At "**5.0**" **DME**, continue descent to "**600**" feet
> 10) You should be at "**600**" feet when the **NAV 1 DME DIST** reads "**3.0**" (This is the **D3.0** fix)
> 11) Set **FLAPS** to **second notch** (20 degrees)
>
> 12) Press "**P**" to pause the simulation

** 13) Record your:

NAV 1 DME DIST_____	(25 pts)
AIRSPEED_____	(20 pts)
VSI_____	(20 pts)
ALTITUDE_____	(20 pts)
HEADING_____	(15 pts)
RPM_____	(15 pts)
CARB HEAT_____	(10 pts)
GEAR_____	(10 pts)

> 14) Press "**P**" to continue the simulation

"Hey! Isn't that a gorgeous sight?!!! I'd say we broke out of the clouds right at 500 feet or so. You are actually flying an instrument approach - that should make you proud as a peacock! Now keep fixing on the runway, but I'll continue to give you the instrument approach instructions."

15) At "**3.0**" **DME**, continue descent to "**440**" feet
16) You need to be at "**440**" feet when **NAV 1 DME DIST** is "**1.7**"
17) Set **FLAPS** to **third notch** (30 degrees)

"All right! Go ahead and adjust to a total visual look at the runway. This will be your night landing, so have fun with it! Relax and wear a big smile on your face - it'll relax the rest of your body!"

18) When **one half** mile from the approach end, airspeed should be "**70**" knots

"The airplane is not a respecter of night or day. It'll still react to the proper corrections, so adjust height with power, and airspeed with pitch."

19) When you are 10 to 20 feet off the runway, reduce power to about "**1000**" RPM, and start to slowly pitch the nose of the aircraft up to slow your descent and establish a touchdown attitude

*"The night time charm! You've got to admit that this is probably one of the most beautiful spots to be in - oh, all right! Sorry to distract you! Is that why your airspeed is starting to scare me a little? WATCH YOUR **AIRSPEED**! Be careful not to stall the aircraft. Don't let your airspeed drop below **60 knots**."*

20) When you are five feet off the runway, hold the nose of the aircraft up and allow the airspeed to **SLOWLY** bleed off. Your aircraft will settle onto the runway while you follow the centerline.

*"Don't be impatient, let the aircraft **settle** onto the runway slowly."*

21) After touchdown, reduce power to **600 RPM**
22) Apply the brakes
23) Turn right and taxi off the active runway
24) When the aircraft stops, set **CARB HEAT** to **"OFF"**
25) Set **FLAPS** to **"0"**

*"You did it! You did an instrument flight and saw how absolutely simple this whole affair can become. Now, it does become much more difficult, but it will feel simple as soon as you learn to talk the instrument language and fly the instrument language. There's a lot of procedural memorization which has to take place, but it's all logical and natural. So, see what you have to look forward to? Let's get our taxi clearance on frequency **121.9**. We'll need some fuel, so let them know that too."*

26) Tune **COM** to **"121.9"** (Kennedy Ground)

You:

"KENNEDY GROUND, CESSNA 13MIKE IS DOWN AND CLEAR OF RUNWAY 22 LEFT FOR TAXI TO THE TERMINAL. WE'LL REQUIRE FUEL, PLEASE."

Kennedy Ground:

"CESSNA 13MIKE, CLEARED TO TAXI TO THE TERMINAL. FUEL TRUCK WILL BE ADVISED OF YOUR NEED."

27) Proceed to the fueling pit on the north side of the tower
28) Turn **LIGHTS "OFF"**
29) Turn **STROBES "OFF"**
30) Turn **MAGS** to **"LEAN"** to shut down the engine
** 31) Record the **TIME** _____(5 pts)

TOTAL POINTS POSSIBLE FOR THIS FLIGHT **510**

12

Answers

Flight Scenario One

FLIGHT PLAN -
 ** a) As you travel from East to West, what VOR do you pass?
  __**PARADISE**__ (15 pts)
 ** b) While heading West, what airport is just to your left?
  __**CORONA**__ (15 pts)
 ** c) What VOR is just south of La Verne?
  __**POMONA**__ (15 pts)

RUN UP -
  ** 3) Select CARB HEAT "**ON**", record RPM drop **80 [50]** (5 pts)
  ** 5) Select "**LEFT**" Mag, record RPM drop __**150 [120]**__ (5 pts)
  ** 7) Select "**RIGHT**" Mag, record RPM drop __**150 [120]**__ (5 pts)

Course change:
  ** 4) Record your:
   NAV 1 DME DIST __**12.7 to 13.1**__ (25 pts)
   NAV 2 DME DIST __**6.7 to 7.0**__ (25 pts)
   ALTITUDE __**4450 to 4550**__ (20 pts)
   AIRSPEED __**125 to 130**__ (15 pts)
   GEAR __**UP**__ (10 pts)
   FLAPS __**UP**__ (10 pts)
   MAGS __**BOTH**__ (10 pts)
   STROBE __**ON**__ (10 pts)
   LIGHTS __**OFF**__ (10 pts)

?

Descent:

   **   5) Record the NAV 2 DME DIST when NAV 1 CDI needle centers __**2.7 - 3.0**__ (25 pts)

Approach:

   **   *"By the way, what would your downwind course be when parallel to runway 26R?"* _____**080**_____ (10 pts)

   **   *"Hey! What is that traffic pattern altitude anyway?"* _____**2000**_____ (15 pts)

   **   2) When established on the DOWNWIND leg of the approach record the heading displayed on your DG __**080**__ (20 pts)

   **   11) Record your:

                  AIRSPEED _____**85 - 90**_____ (25 pts)

                  RPM **1393 to 1408 [1650 to 1750]** (25 pts)

                  VSI _____**-350 to -450**_____ (20 pts)

                  ALTITUDE __**1550 to 1700**__ (20 pts)

                  HEADING _____**165 to 175**_____ (15 pts)

                  CARB HEAT _____**ON**_____ (10 pts)

   **   17) Record your:

                  AIRSPEED _____**65 to 75**_____ (25 pts)

                  VSI _____**-300 to -400**_____ (25 pts)

                  HEADING _____**255 to 265**_____ (20 pts)

                  RPM **1393 to 1408 [1650 to 1750]** (25 pts)

                  FLAPS _____**30 degrees down**_____ (15 pts)

   **   26) Record the **TIME** __**10:25 to 10:35**__ (5 pts)

TOP GUN .... 466 to 495 pts
FLYING LEATHERNECK .... 386 to 465 pts
PROFESSOR CALFIOR'S PROTÉGÉ .... 306 to 385 pts
TEST PILOT HOPEFUL .... 226 to 305 pts
WHITE KNUCKLE WILLIE .... 146 to 225 pts
TAKE THE BUS .... 000 to 145 pts

Flight Scenario Two

FLIGHT PLAN -

** a) What is the altitude of the floor of the TCA where you fly under it?

_____**4000**_____ (15 pts)

** b) What famous horse race track is just North of your route?

_____**Santa Anita Race Track**_____ (15 pts)

** c) What is the name of the airport you fly over?

_____**El Monte**_____ (15 pts)

RUNUP -

** 3) Select CARB HEAT "**ON**", record RPM drop **80 [60]** (5 pts)

** 5) Select "**LEFT**" Mag, record RPM drop **150 [130]** (5 pts)

** 7) Select "**RIGHT**" Mag, record RPM drop **150 [130]** (5 pts)

Course change #1:

** 4) Record your:

NAV 1 DME DIST	**4.1 to 4.3**	(25 pts)
ALTITUDE	**3950 to 4050**	(25 pts)
AIRSPEED	**125 to 130**	(20 pts)
VSI	**-50 to + 50**	(15 pts)
GEAR	**UP**	(10 pts)
FLAPS	**UP**	(10 pts)
MAGS	**BOTH**	(10 pts)
STROBE	**ON**	(5 pts)
LIGHTS	**OFF**	(5 pts)

Altitude change:

** 2) Record your:

ALTITUDE	**3950 to 4050**	(20 pts)
AIRSPEED	**125 to 130**	(20 pts)
VSI	**-50 to +50**	(20 pts)
HEADING	**268 to 272**	(20 pts)

Course change #2:

** 5) Record your:

NAV 1 DME DIST **12.8-13.2 [11.5-11.9]** (25 pts)
NAV 2 DME DIST **13.3-13.7 [12.0-12.4]** (25 pts)
ALTITUDE **4450 to 4550** (20 pts)
AIRSPEED **126 to 134** (20 pts)
VSI **-50 to +50** (15 pts)

Approach:

** 12) Record your:

AIRSPEED **70 to 80** (25 pts)
VSI **350 to 450** (25 pts)
HEADING **210 to 219** (20 pts)
RPM **1390 to 1410 [1650 to 1750]** (15 pts)
FLAPS **30 degrees down** (15 pts)

** 22) Record the **TIME** **12:30 to 12:40** (5 pts)

TOP GUN .... 446 to 475 pts
FLYING LEATHERNECK .... 366 to 445 pts
PROFESSOR CALFIOR'S PROTÉGÉ .... 281 to 365 pts
TEST PILOT HOPEFUL .... 191 to 280 pts
WHITE KNUCKLE WILLIE .... 111 to 190 pts
TAKE THE BUS .... 000 to 110 pts

Flight Scenario Three

FLIGHT PLAN -

** a) What airport is to your left as you leave the LAX TCA Corridor?
COMPTON (15 pts)
** b) How many runways does Los Angeles International have?
4 (15 pts)
** c) What is the height of the floor of the TCA at Santa Monica?
5,000 feet (15 pts)

RUN UP -
*   ** 3) Select CARB HEAT "**ON**", record RPM drop **80 [60]** (5 pts)
*   ** 5) Select "**LEFT**" Mag, record RPM drop __**150 [130]**__ (5 pts)
*   ** 7) Select "**RIGHT**" Mag, record RPM drop __**150 [130]**__ (5 pts)

Takeoff:
*   ** 15) Record your:

ALTITUDE	**2450 to 2850**	(20 pts)
AIRSPEED	**77 to 83**	(20 pts)
VSI	**750 to 850**	(20 pts)
HEADING	**340 to 350**	(15 pts)
FLAPS	**UP**	(10 pts)

CORRIDOR -
*   ** 4) Record your:

NAV 1 DME DIST	**14.2-15.0 [14.9-15.7]**	(25 pts)
NAV 2 DME DIST	**6.3-6.8 [4.9-5.3]**	(25 pts)
ALTITUDE	**3450 to 3550**	(20 pts)
AIRSPEED	**130 to 135**	(15 pts)
XPDR	**3732**	(15 pts)
HEADING	**143 to 148**	(15 pts)
VSI	**-100 to +100**	(15 pts)

Descent:
*   ** 8) Record your:

NAV 1 DME DIST	**22.3 to 23.3**	(25 pts)
NAV 2 DME DIST	**5.5 to 5.8**	(25 pts)
ALTITUDE	**1800 to 2800**	(25 pts)
AIRSPEED	**123 to 130**	(20 pts)
VSI	**-1000 to -1300**	(20 pts)
HEADING	**192 to 198**	(20 pts)

Approach:
*   ** 2) What would be the 45 degree heading to the midfield?
     __**155**__ (20 pts)
*   ** 12) Record your:

AIRSPEED	**85 to 90**	(25 pts)
VSI	**-350 to -450**	(25 pts)
ALTITUDE	**500 to 600**	(25 pts)
RPM	**1384 to 1407 [1650 to 1750]**	(20 pts)

HEADING _____ **195 to 205** _____ (20 pts)
CARB HEAT _____ **ON** _____ (15 pts)

**   18) Record your:
AIRSPEED _____ **65 to 75** _____ (25 pts)
VSI _____ **-350 to -450** _____ (25 pts)
HEADING_____ **285 to 295** _____ (20 pts)
RPM _____ **1384 to 1407   [1650 to 1750]** _____ (15 pts)
FLAPS _____ **30 degrees down** _____ (15 pts)

**   28) Record the **TIME** _____ **12:54 to 13:01** _____ (5 pts)

TOP GUN ....**621 to 665 pts**
FLYING LEATHERNECK ....**516 to 620 pts**
PROFESSOR CALFIOR'S PROTÉGÉ ....**386 to 515 pts**
TEST PILOT HOPEFUL ....**256 to 385 pts**
WHITE KNUCKLE WILLIE ....**126 to 255 pts**
TAKE THE BUS ....**000 to 125 pts**

Flight Scenario Four

FLIGHT PLAN -
**   a) Where can I get a good Buffalo Burger?
_____ **CATALINA ISLAND** _____(15 pts)
**   b) Is the airport North or South of the town of Avalon?
_____ **SOUTH** _____(15 pts)
**   c) What is the altitude of the floor of the TCA at Torrance?
5,000 _____(15 pts)
RUN UP -
**   3) Select CARB HEAT "**ON**", record RPM drop **80 [50]** (5 pts)
**   5) Select "**LEFT**" Mag, record RPM drop ____ **150 [120]** (5 pts)
**   7) Select "**RIGHT**" Mag, record RPM drop ____ **150 [120]** (5 pts)

Climb out:

** *From what you see the needle of your Number 1 VOR doing, which way are your winds coming from - LEFT or RIGHT?"* __RIGHT__ (20 pts)

Level off:

** 5) Record your:

NAV 1 DME DIST __8.2 to 8.6 [4.1 to 4.5]__ (25 pts)
NAV 2 DME DIST __24.7-25.1 [29.0-29.4]__ (25 pts)
ALTITUDE __3450 to 3550__ (20 pts)
AIRSPEED __110 to 120__ (15 pts)
VSI __-50 to +50__ (15 pts)

Approach:

** 5) Record your:

ALTITUDE __2500 to 2650__ (25 pts)
VSI __-50 to +50__ (25 pts)
RPM __1494 to 1508 [1750 to 1850]__ (20 pts)
AIRSPEED __80 to 90__ (20 pts)
HEADING __035 to 045__ (15 pts)
CARB HEAT __ON__ (10 pts)

** 14) Record your:

AIRSPEED __70 to 75__ (20 pts)
VSI __-350 to -450__ (20 pts)
HEADING __217 to 223__ (15 pts)
RPM __1394 to 1409 [1650 to 1750]__ (15 pts)
FLAPS __30 degrees down__ (15 pts)

** 25) Record the **TIME** __13:29 to 13:35__ (5 pts)

TOP GUN .... 366 to 385 pts
FLYING LEATHERNECK .... 301 to 365 pts
PROFESSOR CALFIOR'S PROTÉGÉ .... 231 to 300 pts
TEST PILOT HOPEFUL .... 156 to 230 pts
WHITE KNUCKLE WILLIE .... 091 to 155 pts
TAKE THE BUS .... 000 to 090 pts

Flight Scenario Five

FLIGHT PLAN -

** a) Just before you get to JOLIET VOR what is the name of the airport to your left? ____** Park District**____(15 pts)

** b) What is the name of the VOR just to your left as you depart Lansing? ____** Chicago Heights**____(15 pts)

** c) Do you need to fly under the Chicago TCA any where along your route of flight? ____**NO**____(15 pts)

RUN UP -

** 3) Select CARB HEAT "**ON**", record RPM drop **80 [50]** (5 pts)

** 5) Select "**LEFT**" Mag, record RPM drop____**150 [120]** (5 pts)

** 7) Select "**RIGHT**" Mag, record RPM drop ____**150 [120]** (5 pts)

Course change:

** 1) At "**20**" DME, record your Ground speed **150 to 155**,(25 pts) and heading **268 to 273**, (25 pts) for a centered OBI needle

** 2) How many other airports can you see easily somewhere along your en route track to JOLIET VOR? ____**3**____(15 pts) on the left - __**3**__(15 pts) on the right

** 6) Record your:

NAV 1 DME DIST	**0.7 to 1.2**	(25 pts)
ALTITUDE	**4450 to 4550**	(20 pts)
AIRSPEED	**122 to 128**	(15 pts)
VSI	**-50 to +50**	(15 pts)
GEAR	**UP**	(10 pts)
FLAPS	**UP**	(10 pts)
MAGS	**BOTH**	(10 pts)
STROBE	**ON**	(10 pts)
LIGHTS	**OFF**	(10 pts)

Descent:

** 5) Record your:

NAV 2 DME	**4.2 to 4.7 [5.0 to 5.5]**	(25 pts)
NAV 1 DME	**16.6 to 17.1 [15.8 to 16.3]**	(25 pts)
HEADING	**332 to 340**	(20 pts)
ALTITUDE	**3500 to 3700**	(20 pts)
VSI	**-600 to -800**	(15 pts)
AIRSPEED	**125 to 135**	(15 pts)

** 12) Record your:

NAV 2 DME	**9.0 to 9.7 [9.8 to 10.5]**	(25 pts)
NAV 1 DME	**12.5 to 13.2 [11.5 to 12.2]**	(25 pts)
ALTITUDE	**2350 to 2550**	(20 pts)
AIRSPEED	**125 to 132**	(20 pts)
IS THE FIELD IN SIGHT	**YES**	(15 pts)

Approach:

** 9) Record your:

AIRSPEED	**70 to 80**	(25 pts)
VSI	**-350 to -550**	(25 pts)
HEADING	**355 to 005**	(20 pts)
RPM	**1391 to 1409 [1650 to 1750]**	(20 pts)
FLAPS	**30 degrees down**	(15 pts)
GEAR	**DOWN**	(15 pts)

** 19) Record the **TIME** **10:27 to 10:37** (5 pts)

TOP GUN	576 to 615 pts
FLYING LEATHERNECK	461 to 575 pts
PROFESSOR CALFIOR'S PROTÉGÉ	346 to 460 pts
TEST PILOT HOPEFUL	231 to 345 pts
WHITE KNUCKLE WILLIE	116 to 230 pts
TAKE THE BUS	000 to 115 pts

Flight Scenario Six

FLIGHT PLAN -
** a) What is the name of the airport on the tracks as you cross the 290 radial of Joliet? **WOODLAKE** (15 pts)
** b) What's the name of the river you cross as you head south to Pontiac VOR? **ILLINOIS RIVER** (15 pts)
** c) What interstate do you parallel and cross inbound from Pontiac VOR to your destination? **I 55** (15 pts)

RUN UP -
** 3) Select CARB HEAT "**ON**", record RPM drop **80 [50]** (5 pts)
** 5) Select "**LEFT**" Mag, record RPM drop **150 [120]** (5 pts)
** 7) Select "**RIGHT**" Mag, record RPM drop **150 [120]** (5 pts)

Takeoff:
** 10) At "**700**" feet above the ground, begin a **LEFT** "**90**" degree CROSSWIND turn; What altitude is that? **1400** (20 pts)

** 12) Your heading for the CROSSWIND leg is **270** (15 pts)
Your heading for the DOWNWIND leg is **180** (15 pts)

Pattern Departure:
** 2) Record the heading displayed on your DG **177 to 183** (20 pts)
Record the altitude you're passing **2800 to 2900** (15 pts)

** 3) At midfield, turn RIGHT "**45**" degrees, maintaining the climb. What will that heading be? **225** (15 pts)

Level off:

** 5) Record your:

NAV 1 DME DIST <u>15.3-15.7 [14.9-15.3]</u> (25 pts)
HEADING <u>220 to 230</u> (20 pts)
RPM <u>2240 to 2260 [2400 to 2500]</u> (20 pts)
AIRSPEED <u>115 to 125</u> (15 pts)
GEAR <u>UP</u> (10 pts)
FLAPS <u>UP</u> (10 pts)

Course change #1:

** 3) Record your:

NAV 1 DME DIST <u>17.7-18.2 [16.2-16.7]</u> (25 pts)
ALTITUDE <u>2950 to 3050</u> (20 pts)
NAV 2 DME DIST <u>48.0-48.5 [49.1-49.6]</u> (20 pts)

Course change #2:

** 6) Record your:

NAV 1 DME DIST <u>50.5-51.0 [53.6-54.1]</u> (25 pts)
NAV 2 DME DIST <u>33.3-33.8 [33.5-34.0]</u> (25 pts)
AIRSPEED <u>126 to 134</u> (20 pts)
HEADING <u>166 to 170</u> (20 pts)

Approach:

** 1) When abeam a point on the runway between the departure end of runway 11 and midfield, begin a **RIGHT** turn to the DOWNWIND leg. Heading <u>290</u> (20 pts)

** 6) When the end of the runway is at your 5 o'clock position, turn **LEFT** "**90**" degrees to establish your BASE leg of the approach. Heading <u>200</u> (20 pts)

** 9) Record your:

AIRSPEED <u>80 to 90</u> (25 pts)
VSI <u>-300 to -500</u> (25 pts)
ALTITUDE <u>1350 to 1450</u> (20 pts)
HEADING <u>195 to 205</u> (20 pts)

RPM	**1490 to 1510 [1750 to 1850]**	(20 pts)
CARB HEAT	**ON**	(10 pts)
LIGHTS	**OFF**	(10 pts)
GEAR	**DOWN**	(10 pts)

** 14) Record your:

AIRSPEED	**70 to 80**	(25 pts)
VSI	**-350 to -450**	(20 pts)
HEADING	**105 to 115**	(20 pts)
RPM	**1490 to 1510 [1750 to 1850]**	(20 pts)
FLAPS	**30 degrees down**	(15 pts)

** 24) Record the **TIME**   **12:47 to 12:55**   (5 pts)

TOP GUN	661 to 700 pts
FLYING LEATHERNECK	551 to 660 pts
PROFESSOR CALFIOR'S PROTÉGÉ	436 to 550 pts
TEST PILOT HOPEFUL	326 to 435 pts
WHITE KNUCKLE WILLIE	216 to 325 pts
TAKE THE BUS	000 to 215 pts

Flight Scenario Seven

FLIGHT PLAN -

** a) How many Victor Airways converge at Roberts VOR?
_____**8**_____(15 pts)

** b) What major road parallels your track from Roberts VOR to Kankakee?   **I 57**_____(15 pts)

** c) What is the name of the private airstrip on the right halfway between Roberts and Kankakee_____**CLASSEN**_____(15 pts)

RUN UP -
      ** 3) Select CARB HEAT "**ON**", record RPM drop **80 [60]** (5 pts)
      ** 5) Select "**LEFT**" Mag, record RPM drop **150 [130]** (5 pts)
      ** 7) Select "**RIGHT**" Mag, record RPM drop **150 [130]** (5 pts)

Takeoff:
      ** 9) At "**500**" feet above the ground, raise the flaps to "0".
          What is your altitude? **1400** (20 pts)
      ** 10) At "**1000**" feet above the ground, make a "**45**" degree right
          departure turn. What is that desired heading? **075** (20 pts)
      ** 13) Record your:

NAV 1 DME DIST **2.2 to 2.4 [1.7 to 1.9]**	(25 pts)
ALTITUDE **2200 to 2400**	(20 pts)
AIRSPEED **80 to 85**	(15 pts)
VSI **600 to 800**	(15 pts)
GEAR **UP**	(10 pts)
FLAPS **UP**	(10 pts)

To ROBERTS VOR:
      ** 4) Record your:

Ground speed from NAV 2 **108 to 115**	(20 pts)
NAV 2 DME DIST **24.5 to 24.8 [25.2 to 25.5]**	(25 pts)
NAV 2 COURSE with centered needle	
088 to 092 [080 to 084]	(25 pts)
Airspeed **126 to 133**	(20 pts)
ROBERTS VOR **12 to 13**	(20 pts)

Course change #1:
      ** 3) From the above, what might be a **good heading** to go to?
          035 to 045 (20 pts)

Descent:
      ** 5) Record your:

NAV 1 DME DIST **23.6 to 23.9 [N/A]**	(25 pts)
ALTITUDE **3450 to 3550**	(20 pts)
HEADING **035 to 045**	(20 pts)
AIRSPEED **126 to 134**	(15 pts)

Traffic pattern entry:
      ** 2) Heading **165** (20 pts)

?

**   4) Heading _____**265**_____(20 pts)

**   6) Record your:

            NAV 1 DME DIST __**4.4 to 4.9 [N/A]**__ (25 pts)
            ALTITUDE _____**2300 to 2400**___ (20 pts)
            RIGHT DOWNWIND HEADING __**220**__ (20 pts)
            CARB HEAT _____**ON**_____ (10 pts)
            CURRENT HEADING __**260 to 270**___ (10 pts)

Approach:

**   8) Adjust height with _____** Power**_____(20 pts)

    9) Adjust airspeed with _____**Pitch**_____(20 pts)

**   13) Record your:

            AIRSPEED _____**75 to 85**_____ (25 pts)
            ALTITUDE _____**1100 to 1250**_____ (25 pts)
            RPM __**1350 to 1420 [1650 to 1750]**___ (20 pts)
            HEADING _____**305 to 315**_____ (20 pts)
            VSI _____**-350 to -450**_____ (15 pts)
            CARB HEAT _____**ON**_____ (15 pts)
            GEAR _____**DOWN**_____ (10 pts)

**   19) Record your:

            AIRSPEED _____**70 to 80**_____ (20 pts)
            VSI _____**-300 to -500**_____ (20 pts)
             HEADING _____**035 to 045**_____ (15 pts)
            RPM __**1200 to 1400 [1500 to 1700]**___ (15 pts)
            FLAPS _____**30 degrees down**_____ (10 pts)

**   28) Record the **TIME** ___**14:17 to 14:25**___ (5 pts)

TOP GUN ....736 to 785 pts
FLYING LEATHERNECK ....606 to 735 pts
PROFESSOR CALFIOR'S PROTÉGÉ ....471 to 605 pts
TEST PILOT HOPEFUL ....341 to 470 pts
WHITE KNUCKLE WILLIE ....211 to 340 pts
TAKE THE BUS ....000 to 210 pts

Flight Scenario Eight

FLIGHT PLAN -

**   a) About a minute or two prior to reaching abeam of Sanger Field, you bypass a tower whose elevation is how many feet mean sea level (MSL)_____**1236**_____(15 pts)

**   b) What airport to the east should you see as you proceed to Meigs Field from Chicago Heights?_____** Gary Regional**_____(15 pts)

**   c) What is the name of the Airport Radar Service Area (ARSA) that's to your left as you fly inbound to Meigs Field?**Chicago Midway**(15 pts)

RUN UP -

**   3) Select CARB HEAT "**ON**", record RPM drop__**80 [50]**_(5 pts)

**   5) Select "**LEFT**" Mag, record RPM drop_____**150 [120]**_(5 pts)

**   7) Select "**RIGHT**" Mag, record RPM drop ___**150 [120]**_(5 pts)

Course change:

**   5) Record your:

GROUND SPEED	**108 to 115**	(20 pts)
NAV 1 DME DIST	**9.5 to 10.1 [10.5-11.1]**	(25 pts)
ALTITUDE	**3450 to 3550**	(20 pts)
NAV 1 CDI HEADING	**058 to 062**	(25 pts)
AIRSPEED	**125 to 134**	(15 pts)
VSI	**-50 to +50**	(15 pts)

Descent:

**   9) Record your:

NAV 2 DME	**7.6 to 8.1 [8.6 to 9.1]**	(25 pts)
HEADING	**360 to 005**	(20 pts)
ALTITUDE	**1800 to 2000**	(20 pts)
AIRSPEED	**110 to 129**	(15 pts)
VSI	**-450 to -550**	(15 pts)

?

Approach:

** 8) Record your:

AIRSPEED_____**70 to 80**_____ (25 pts)
VSI_____**-400 to -600**_____ (20 pts)
HEADING_____**352 to 005**_____ (15 pts)
RPM____**1350 to 1510 [1650 to 1850]**____ (15 pts)
FLAPS_____**30 degrees down**_____ (10 pts)
GEAR_____**DOWN**_____ (10 pts)

** 20) Record the **TIME** _____**15:35 to 15:45**_____ (5 pts)

TOP GUN ....351 to 375 pts
FLYING LEATHERNECK ....291 to 350 pts
PROFESSOR CALFIOR'S PROTÉGÉ ....221 to 290 pts
TEST PILOT HOPEFUL ....151 to 220 pts
WHITE KNUCKLE WILLIE ....086 to 150 pts
TAKE THE BUS ....000 to 085 pts

Flight Scenario Nine

FLIGHT PLAN -

** a) What is the name of the airport to your right, about 20 miles into the flight? _____**HOLLISTER**_____(15 pts)

** b) What is the height of the mountain to your left, as you turn towards San Jose? _____**4400**_____(15 pts)

** c) What is the name of the mountain in question "b"?
_____**Mt. Hamilton**_____(15 pts)

RUN UP -

** 3) Select CARB HEAT "**ON**", record RPM drop__**80 [50]**__(5 pts)

** 5) Select "**LEFT**" Mag, record RPM drop_____**150 [120]**__(5 pts)

** 7) Select "**RIGHT**" Mag, record RPM drop ____**150 [120]**__(5 pts)

Takeoff:

** 13) Record your:

ALTITUDE	1550 to 1750	(25 pts)
HEADING	345 to 355	(20 pts)
AIRSPEED	75 to 85	(15 pts)
VSI	950 to 1150	(15 pts)
FLAPS	UP	(15 pts)

Course:

** 5) Record your:

ALTITUDE	3450 to 3550	(25 pts)
AIRSPEED	125 to 132	(20 pts)
VSI	-50 to +50	(20 pts)
HEADING	186 to 196	(15 pts)
RPM	2096 to 2204 [2250 to 2450]	(15 pts)

Approach:

** 13) What is your heading for the base leg? __220__ (20 pts)

** 14) Will you land with a LEFT or a RIGHT crosswind?
____**LEFT**____ (20 pts)

** 15) Have you been cleared to land yet? ____** No**____ (20 pts)

** 18) Record your:

ALTITUDE	550 to 700	(25 pts)
AIRSPEED	75 to 85	(20 pts)
VSI	-400 to -600	(20 pts)
HEADING	185 to 205	(25 pts)
CARB HEAT	ON	(20 pts)
RPM	1200 to 1407 [1500 to 1750]	(20 pts)
FLAPS	20 degrees DOWN	(15 pts)

** 23) Record your:

AIRSPEED	65 to 75	(25 pts)
VSI	-350 to -500	(25 pts)
HEADING	115 to 130	(20 pts)

RPM   <u>**1200 to 1350 [1500 to 1650]**</u>   (20 pts)
FLAPS   <u>**30 degrees DOWN**</u>   (15 pts)
GEAR   <u>**DOWN**</u>   (15 pts)

**   32) Record the **TIME**   <u>**18:41 to 18:49**</u>   (5 pts)

TOP GUN .... 546 to 575 pts
FLYING LEATHERNECK .... 441 to 545 pts
PROFESSOR CALFIOR'S PROTÉGÉ .... 331 to 440 pts
TEST PILOT HOPEFUL .... 221 to 330 pts
WHITE KNUCKLE WILLIE .... 111 to 220 pts
TAKE THE BUS .... 000 to 110 pts

Flight Scenario Ten

FLIGHT PLAN -
   **   a) What VOR do you fly over before you reach the coast?
    <u>**Woodside**</u> (15 pts)
   **   b) What is the name of the airport you will fly over on the coast?
    <u>**Half Moon Bay**</u> (15 pts)
   **   c) When you are lined up to land at Oakland, what airport will be
     to your left? <u>**NAS ALAMEDA**</u> (15 pts)

RUN UP -
   **   3) Select CARB HEAT "**ON**", record RPM drop <u>**80 [50]**</u> (5 pts)
   **   5) Select "**LEFT**" Mag, record RPM drop <u>**150 [120]**</u> (5 pts)
   **   7) Select "**RIGHT**" Mag, record RPM drop <u>**150 [120]**</u> (5 pts)

Takeoff:
   **   *"You should see the runway out the right window. Remember to tell*
     tower that you're passing through 1100 feet - they just want to make
     sure you're clear of the pattern altitude. You should be flying parallel to
     the runway heading, so what heading is that?" <u>**290**</u> (20 pts)

**   14) Record your:

NAV 1 DME DIST   **14.6-15.1 [15.6-16.1]**   (25 pts)
ALTITUDE   **2200 to 2500**   (20 pts)
HEADING   **242 to 248**   (20 pts)
AIRSPEED   **75 to 85**   (15 pts)
VSI   **750 to 900**   (15 pts)
GEAR   **UP**   (10 pts)
FLAPS   **UP**   (10 pts)
MAGS   **BOTH**   (10 pts)
STROBE   **ON**   (10 pts)
LIGHTS   **ON**   (10 pts)

Course change:

**   4) Record your:

NAV 1 DME DIST   **5.8-6.2 [5.4-5.8]**   (25 pts)
NAV 2 DME DIST **45.8-46.4 [48.2-48.8]** (25 pts)
ALTITUDE   **4450 to 4550**   (20 pts)
AIRSPEED   **124 to 134**   (15 pts)

Approach:

**   5) Record your:

AIRSPEED   **100 to 110**   (25 pts)
RPM   **1390 to 1410 [1650 to 1750]**   (25 pts)
VSI   **-400 to -600**   (20 pts)
ALTITUDE   **1350 to 1550**   (20 pts)
HEADING   **090 to 105**   (15 pts)
CARB HEAT   **ON**   (10 pts)
XPDR   **4451**   (10 pts)

**   14) Record your:

AIRSPEED   **75 to 85**   (25 pts)
RPM   **1390 to 1410 [1650 to 1750]**   (25 pts)
VSI   **-400 to -600**   (20 pts)
ALTITUDE   **500 to 700**   (20 pts)
HEADING   **100 to 120**   (15 pts)
CARB HEAT   **ON**   (10 pts)
GEAR   **DOWN**   (10 pts)

?

**   18) Record your:

AIRSPEED	**70 to 80**	(25 pts)
VSI	**-400 to -600**	(25 pts)
HEADING	**105 to 115**	(20 pts)
RPM	**1350 to 1410 [1650 to 1750]**	(25 pts)
FLAPS	**30 degrees DOWN**	(15 pts)

**   28) Record the **TIME**   **21:32 to 21:36**   (5 pts)

TOP GUN . . . . 641 to 675 pts
FLYING LEATHERNECK . . . . 516 to 640 pts
PROFESSOR CALFIOR'S PROTÉGÉ . . . . 386 to 515 pts
TEST PILOT HOPEFUL . . . . 256 to 385 pts
WHITE KNUCKLE WILLIE . . . . 126 to 255 pts
TAKE THE BUS . . . . 000 to 125 pts

Flight Scenario Eleven

FLIGHT PLAN -
**   a) What is the name of the body of water you will be crossing from
          Connecticut to the New York side?__**Long Island Sound**__ (15 pts)
**   b) What airspace do you just miss as you turn inbound toward the
          Kennedy VOR?_____**Long Island ARSA**_____(15 pts)
**   c) What river will you be heading north on to arrive at La Guardia
          Airport?_____**Hudson River**_____(15 pts)

RUN UP -
**   3) Select CARB HEAT "**ON**", record RPM drop__**80 [60]**__(5 pts)
**   5) Select "**LEFT**" Mag, record RPM drop_____**150   [130]**__(5 pts)
**   7) Select "**RIGHT**" Mag, record RPM drop ___**150   [130]**__(5 pts)

Climb out:

** 5) Maintain your DOWNWIND heading _____ **240** _____ (20 pts)
   until the **NAV 1 CDI** needle **centers**

Course change:

** 1) When level at "**6000**", record your Ground speed **108 to 114
   [N/A] (20** pts), and heading for a centered CDI needle **214
   to 218** (20 pts)

** 5) Record your:

NAV 2 DME DIST	**32.2-32.6 [28.8-30.2]**	(25 pts)
ALTITUDE	**5950 to 6050**	(20 pts)
AIRSPEED	**124 to 132**	(20 pts)
COM FREQUENCY	**124.5**	(20 pts)
XPDR CODE	**2323**	(20 pts)

** 16) Record your:

NAV 2 DME	**14.1-14.5 [14.8-15.2]**	(25 pts)
NAV 1 DME	**16.0-16.4 [16.3-16.7]**	(25 pts)
ALTITUDE	**3950 to 4050**	(20 pts)
AIRSPEED	**126 to 134**	(15 pts)
VSI	**-50 to +50**	(15 pts)
HEADING	**242 to 250**	(15 pts)

Approach:

** 16) Record your:

AIRSPEED	**85 to 95**	(25 pts)
VSI	**-400 to -600**	(25 pts)
ALTITUDE	**1700 to 1850**	(20 pts)
HEADING	**135 to 150**	(15 pts)
CARB HEAT	**ON**	(15 pts)
RPM	**1390 to 1540 [1700 to 1850]**	(15 pts)
GEAR	**DOWN**	(15 pts)

**   22) Record your:

AIRSPEED_____**75 to 85**____   (25 pts)

VSI_____**-500 to -800**___   (25 pts)

**   31) Record the **TIME** _____**10:54 to 11:02**____   (5 pts)

TOP GUN	491 to 525 pts
FLYING LEATHERNECK	401 to 490 pts
PROFESSOR CALFIOR'S PROTÉGÉ	306 to 400 pts
TEST PILOT HOPEFUL	211 to 305 pts
WHITE KNUCKLE WILLIE	116 to 210 pts
TAKE THE BUS	000 to 115 pts

Flight Scenario Twelve

FLIGHT PLAN -

**   a) What airport is just on the other side of the New York/Connecticut border by Carmel VOR?_____** Danbury**_____(15 pts)

**   b) What are the ATIS frequencies for Kennedy? **115.4 or 117.7** (15 pts)

**   c) What is the name of the NDB that is at the departure end of runway 22 at Kennedy?_____**CONDA**_____(15 pts)

PREFLIGHT -

What was the name of JFK International originally?
_____**Idlewild**_____*(20 pts).*

What was the name of the stadium where the New York Mets used to play? _____**Shea**_____*(20 pts)*

RUN UP -

**   3) Select CARB HEAT "**ON**", record RPM drop__**80 [50]** (5 pts)

**   5) Select "**LEFT**" Mag, record RPM drop_____**150 [120]** (5 pts)

**   7) Select "**RIGHT**" Mag, record RPM drop ____**150 [120]** (5 pts)

Course changes:

   **   4) Record your:

           GROUND SPEED **120 to 130** (25 pts)

           NAV 2 DME DIST **10.8-11.3 [13.3-13.8]** (25 pts)

           ALTITUDE **4950 to 5050** (20 pts)

           AIRSPEED **126 to 134** (20 pts)

           CURRENT HEADING **160 to 175** (20 pts)

           COM FREQUENCY **119.8** (20 pts)

           RPM **2190 to 2210 [2350 to 2450]** (15 pts)

Descent:

   **   10) Record your:

           NAV 2 DME **29.6-30.3 [28.6-29.3]** (25 pts)

           ADF Needle Position **10 left to 10 right** (25 pts)

           AIRSPEED **135 to 145** (20 pts)

           VSI **-600 to -1500** (20 pts)

           RPM **2090 to 2110 [2250 to 2350]** (20 pts)

           HEADING **195 to 205** (15 pts)

Approach:

   **   13) Record your:

           NAV 1 DME DIST **2.8 to 2.9** (25 pts)

           AIRSPEED **80 to 90** (20 pts)

           VSI **0 to -500** (20 pts)

           ALTITUDE **550 to 650** (20 pts)

           HEADING **218 to 227** (15 pts)

           RPM **1450 to 1550 [1750 to 1850]** (15 pts)

           CARB HEAT **ON** (10 pts)

           GEAR **DOWN** (10 pts)

   **   31) Record the **TIME** **20:00 to 20:08** (5 pts)

TOP GUN	**481 to 510 pts**
FLYING LEATHERNECK	**401 to 480 pts**
PROFESSOR CALFIOR'S PROTÉGÉ	**311 to 400 pts**
TEST PILOT HOPEFUL	**221 to 310 pts**
WHITE KNUCKLE WILLIE	**131 to 220 pts**
TAKE THE BUS	**000 to 130 pts**

APPENDIX A

Flight plan form

FLIGHT PLAN

1. TYPE	2. AIRCRAFT IDENTIFICATION	3. AIRCRAFT TYPE/ SPECIAL EQUIPMENT	4. TRUE AIRSPEED	5. DEPARTURE POINT	6. DEPARTURE TIME		7. CRUISING ALTITUDE
					PROPOSED (Z)	ACTUAL (Z)	
IFR							
VFR			KNOTS				
DVFR							

8. ROUTE OF FLIGHT

9. DESTINATION (Name of airport and city)	10. EST. TIME EN ROUTE		11. REMARKS
	HOURS	MINUTES	

12. FUEL ON BOARD		13. ALTERNATE AIRPORT(S)	14. PILOT'S NAME, ADDRESS, TELEPHONE NO. AND AIRCRAFT HOME BASE	15. NO. ABOARD
HOURS	MINUTES			

16. COLOR OF AIRCRAFT

CLOSE FLIGHT PLAN WITH _____ FSS

A

Flight plan worksheet

NAVIGATION LOG

Aircraft Number N _____

Notes _____

Check Points (Fixed)	VOR Ident Freq.	Course (Route)	Altitude	Wind Dir/Vel — Temp.	CAS — TAS	TC — L R WCA	TH — E W Var	MH — Dev	CH	Dist — Leg Rem	GS Est. Act.	Time off — ETE ETA ATE — GPH Fuel Rem ATA
Totals △												

Airport & ATIS Advisories

	Departure	Destination
ATIS Code		
Ceiling/Vis		
Winds		
Altimeter		
Approach		
Runway		
Time Check		

Airport Frequencies

	Departure	Destination
ATIS		
FSS		
Apch / Grnd		
Tower		
Dep. / Grnd		
UNICOM		

Block In	
Block Out	
Log Time	

APPENDIX B

Chicago Sectional

The map for the Chicago flight scenarios is in two parts. The first part covering the Northern area is on pages 254 and 255. The Southern area is on pages 256 and 257. The distance between latitude lines is 30 miles. Study the sectionals, there is a wealth of information on them. All the map sections overlap and are to scale. (see Figure B.1)

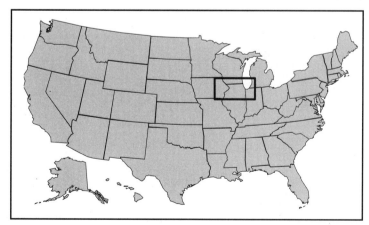

Figure B.1.

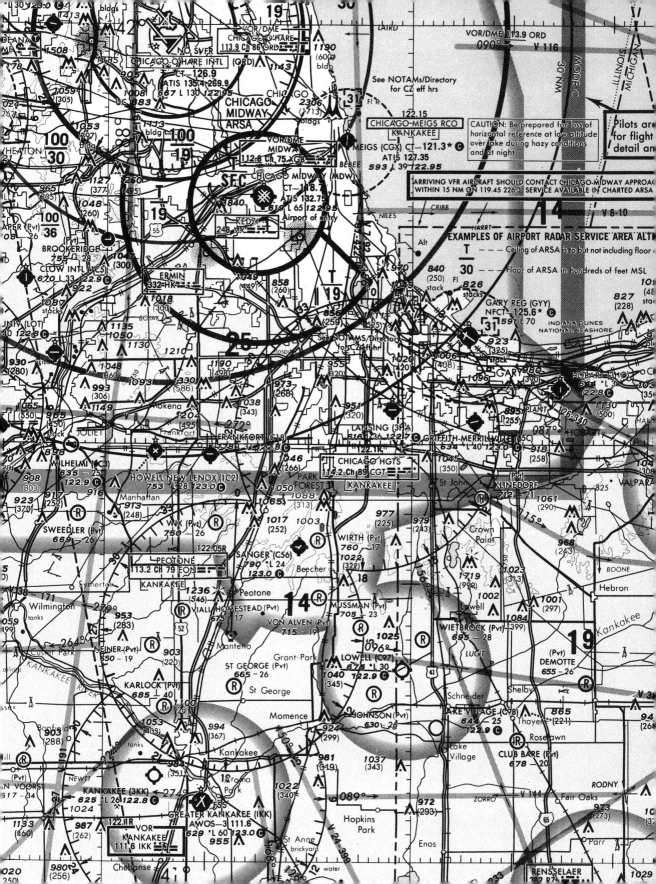

Los Angeles Sectional

The map for the Los Angeles flight scenarios is in two parts. The first part covering the Northern area is on pages 260 and 261. The Southern area is on pages 262 and 263. The distance between latitude lines is 30 miles. Study the sectionals, there is a wealth on information on them. All the map sections overlap and are to scale. (see Figure B.2)

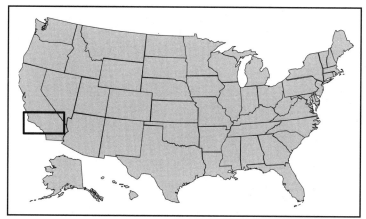

Figure B.2.

B

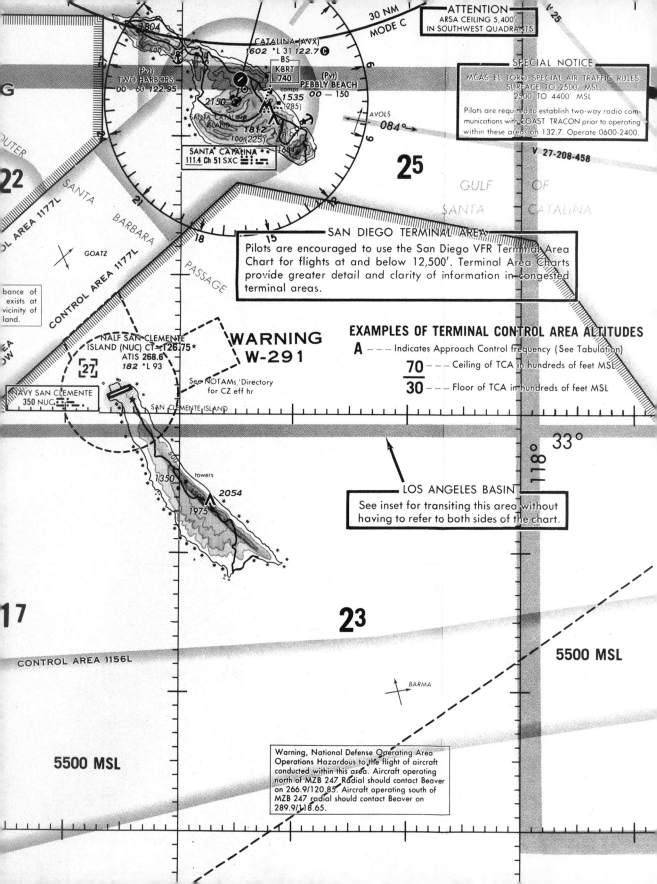

30 NM
MODE C

CATALINA (AVX)
1602 *L 31 122.7 **C**

BS
KBRT
740
PEBBLY BEACH
(Pvt)
00 — 150

(Pvt)
TWO HARBORS
00 — 60 122.95

1804

2150

comps
1535
(285)

SANTA CATALINA
ISLAND

1812
100r(225)

1684

AVOLS
084°

SANTA CATALINA
111.4 Ch 51 SXC

25

V 27-208-458

GULF OF
SANTA   CATALINA

SANTA
BARBARA

PASSAGE

GOATZ

CONTROL AREA 1177L

bance of
exists at
vicinity of
land.

SAN DIEGO TERMINAL AREA
Pilots are encouraged to use the San Diego VFR Terminal Area Chart for flights at and below 12,500'. Terminal Area Charts provide greater detail and clarity of information in congested terminal areas.

**WARNING
W-291**

NALF SAN CLEMENTE
ISLAND (NUC) CT 126.75 *
ATIS 268.6
182 *L 93

27

See NOTAMs, Directory
for CZ eff hr

NAVY SAN CLEMENTE
350 NUC

SAN CLEMENTE ISLAND

EXAMPLES OF TERMINAL CONTROL AREA ALTITUDES
A – – – Indicates Approach Control frequency (See Tabulation)
$\dfrac{70}{30}$ – – – Ceiling of TCA in hundreds of feet MSL
$\dfrac{}{}$ – – – Floor of TCA in hundreds of feet MSL

1350

towers

2054

1975

118° **33°**

LOS ANGELES BASIN
See inset for transiting this area without having to refer to both sides of the chart.

17

23

CONTROL AREA 1156L

5500 MSL

BARMA

5500 MSL

New York Sectional

The map for the New York flight scenarios is in two parts. The first part covering the Northern area is on pages 266 and 267. The Southern area is on pages 268 and 269. The distance between latitude lines is 30 miles. Study the sectionals, there is a wealth on information on them. All the map sections overlap and are to scale. (see Figure B.3)

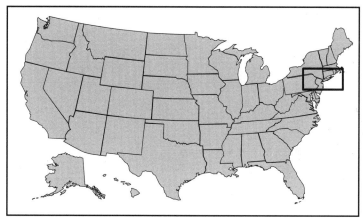

Figure B.3.

B

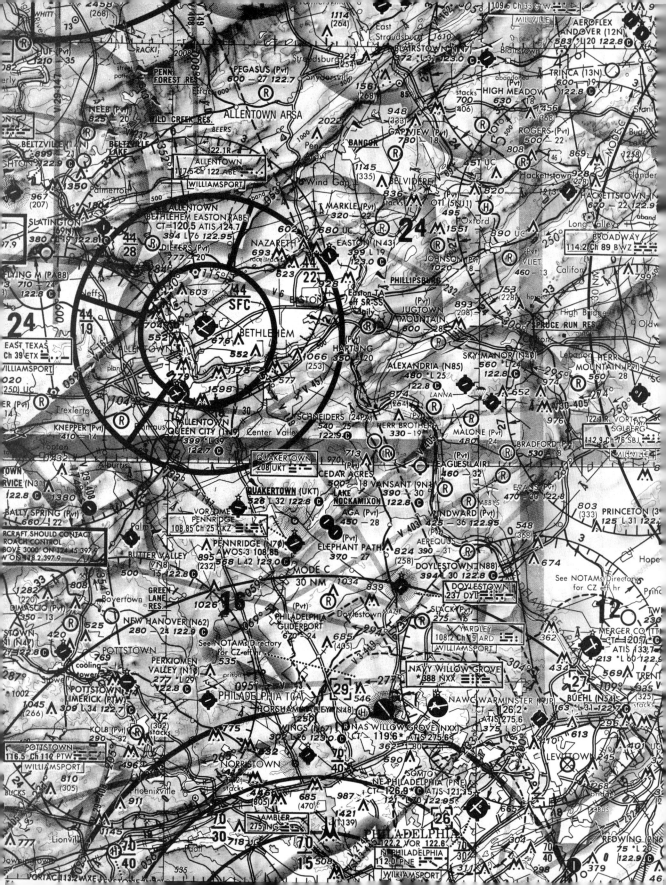

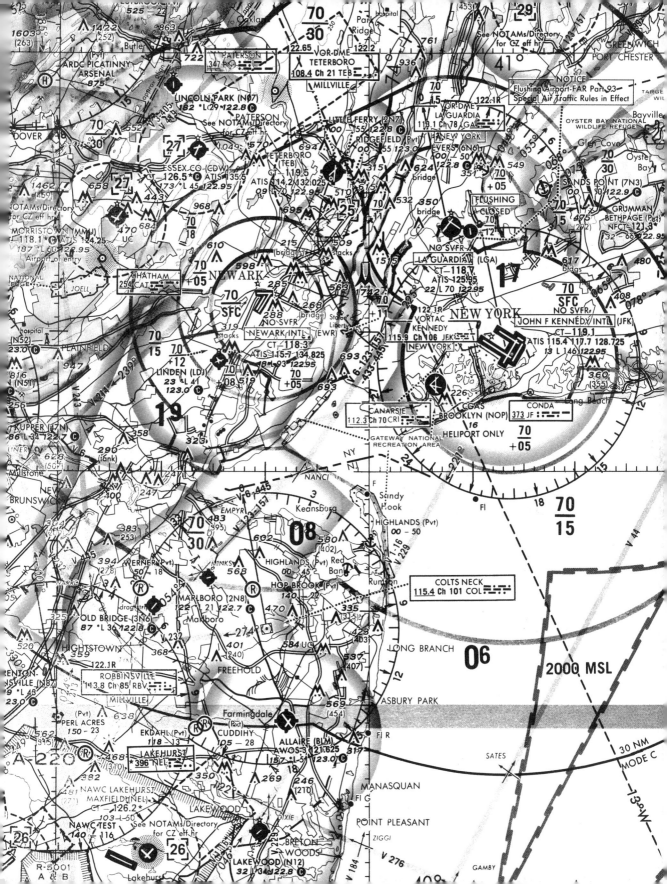

San Francisco Sectional

The map for the San Francisco flight scenarios is in two parts. The first part covering the Northern area is on pages 272 and 273. The Southern area is on pages 274 and 275. The distance between latitude lines is 30 miles. Study the sectionals, there is a wealth of information on them. All the map sections overlap and are to scale. (see Figure B.4)

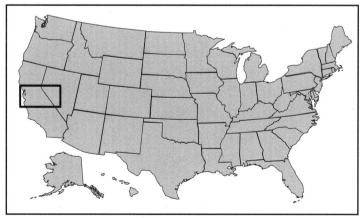

Figure B.4.

B

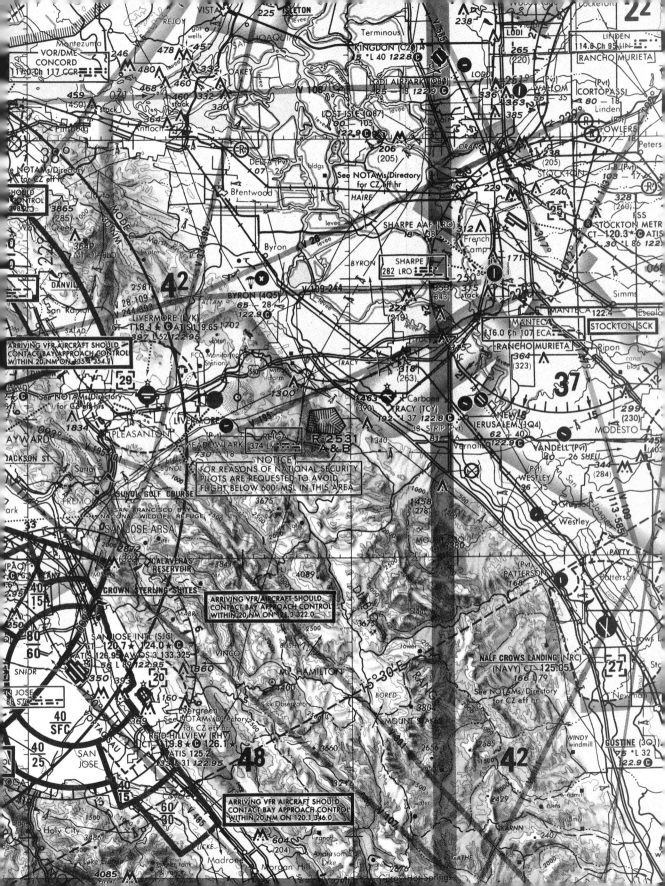

Order Form

Upcoming Books

IFR Flights of "13MIKE" .... $19.95(March)
Airienteering with "13MIKE" .... $19.95 (June)

Now Available

Flights of "13MIKE" $19.95

To Order Books

Quantity	Title	Unit Price	Total
_____	_____	_____	_____
_____	_____	_____	_____
_____	_____	_____	_____

"Quantity Discounts Available"   Subtotal _____
                                 5% Sales Tax (Arizona only) _____
                               Shipping and Handling ($3.99) _____
                                            TOTAL ORDER _____

How to Order

Credit card orders please call (602)778-1245.   Monday - Friday 9 to 5 MST.
To mail: Please remit a copy of the following form, with payment, to:

Calmil Publishing, 2224 Katahn, Prescott, AZ   86301-3976

Name:_____

Address:_____

City:_____State:_____Zip:_____

Visa/MC#:_____Exp. date:_____

Signature:_____

Order Form